Techniques of Gem Cutting
A Lapidary Manual

Techniques of Gem Cutting:

A Lapidary Manual

HERBERT SCARFE

Watson-Guptill Publications

First published in the United States in 1966 by Watson–Guptill
Publications, a division of Billboard Publications, Inc.,
One Astor Plaza, New York, New York 10036

Copyright © 1975 by Herbert Scarfe
First published in 1975 in Great Britain

Manufactured in Great Britain

Library of Congress Cataloging in Publication Data
Scarfe, Herbert.
  Techniques of gem cutting.

  Bibliography: p.
  1. Gem cutting.   I. Title.
TS752.5.S28 1976   736'.2'028   75-6993
ISBN 0-8230-5095-5

ACKNOWLEDGMENT

I am grateful to my wife Doreen for her encouragement and total involvement in the preparation of this book, also to my son Douglas and Eric Johnson of Hull for taking photographs of working sequences. Thanks are due to Trevor Kirk for the photograph of his workshop; to John F. Turner, Glenjoy Lapidary Supplies, Wakefield, for his helpful advice and photographs of examples from his private collection. Additional items photographed were kindly loaned by Joe Bradley of Derwent Crafts, York.

I am also indebted to Dennis Durham, Guy Wilson and 'Taff' Rowberry, members of Kingston Lapidary Society, Hull, for allowing samples of their work to be included, and to Albert Lutman of York for permission to illustrate his mud saw.

Acknowledgment is made to the following by whose courtesy their photographs are reproduced:

His Grace, the Duke of Atholl, Blair Castle, Scotland, figures 3, 4
The Trustees, British Museum, London, figure 2
The Controller, Her Majesty's Stationery Office, figures 127, 147
Whitby Literary and Philosophical Society, figure 5
Kunsthistorisches Museum, Vienna, figure 1
Ammonite Limited, Cowbridge, Glamorgan, figure 17
Carborundum Company, Manchester, England, figure 7
H. C. Evans & Son, London, figures 16, 19
Griffin & George Ltd, Technical Studies, Wembley, Middlesex, figure 20
A. and D. Hughes, Warley, Worcestershire, figure 28
Kernowcraft Rocks and Gems Ltd, Truro, Cornwall, figures 24, 30
Minerals and Gemstones, Penzance, Cornwall, figure 15
PMR Lapidary Equipment and Supplies, Pitlochry, Scotland, figure 18
Diamond Pacific Tool Corporation, Barstow, California, figures 12, 23
Geode Industries Inc, New London, Iowa, figures 29, 32, 99
Highland Park Manufacturing, Division of Musto Industries Inc,
    Hawthorne, California, figures 14, 17, 31
Lortone Division, The Carborundum Company, Seattle, Washington,
    figure 26
Ran-co Products, Granada Hills, California, figures 22, 69
Star Diamond Industries Inc, Division of Craftool Company, Inc,
    Harbor City, California, figure 21

The help and courtesy received from manufacturers and suppliers of lapidary equipment is greatly appreciated.

Herbert Scarfe
Long Riston 1975

Contents

1 The Art of the Lapidary

What do we mean by lapidary? In the accepted sense lapidary relates to the cutting of stones, especially precious stones, and also to the cutter applying his skills to fashion the raw material into gemstones for use in jewellery. Finer distinctions have isolated the lapidary working in semi-precious and coloured stones from the more exalted status of the diamond cutter. To confine lapidary within any narrow field is to ignore our past heritage where craftsmen of earlier cultures cut and polished stones with such skill and artistry that many examples rate highly among the world's fine-art treasures. Histories of lapidary and allied crafts are recorded in several comprehensive books, and chroniclers have left a wealth of technical knowledge and contemporary lore associated with gemstones. However, in some cases names and descriptions recorded of many precious stones are no longer applied to the stones as we know them today and down the centuries 'precious' can only be a relative term.

Much lapidary art of the past had a religious significance and was often associated with mythology and folk lore. Outstanding carvings of ancient deities, ceremonial and ritualistic artifacts, have survived from Mexican and Oriental cultures, utilizing such materials as jade, rock crystal, obsidian and turquoise which were superbly cut and finished. Among the earliest stones carved and engraved were cylindrical seals cut intaglio to form impressions in clay and wax as signatures and proof of ownership. These were carved from a variety of stones and drilled with a hollow core for threading on a cord or thong. Throughout Egyptian dynasties lapidaries and jewellers were held in high esteem and articles fashioned in gold, silver and other metals included rings, bracelets and necklaces, both hand-wrought and cast, set with polished stones. The art of inlaying precious stones, ivory and mother-of-pearl in metals and wood was widely practised. Scarabs evolved as flat seals and decorative items of adornment embellished with personal symbols and were used as amulets or charms against evil. The scarab forms of sacred beetles were cut in domed profile and engraved intaglio or carved in relief portraying a range of pictorial symbols incorporating animals, plants, birds and human forms. The prolific output of these objects can be appreciated through the extensive displays to be seen in museums today. Stones used during these periods included amethyst, agate, carnelian, chalcedony emerald, garnet, jasper, lapis-lazuli, onyx, turquoise, rock crystal, obsidian and haematite. Basalt, porphyry, alabaster, marble, granite, slate and limestone were also used for both small and large sculptures.

Greek and Roman lapidary arts flourished with demands for seals, amulets and commemorative ornaments with subjects based on cult and sacrificial themes, legends of gods, heroes and demons. Figure groups and portraiture became popular, cut as

Figure 1. Sardonyx cameo 'Gemma Augustea' Greco-Roman 12 AD (courtesy of Kunsthistorisches Museum, Vienna)

cameos and intaglios for seals and jewellery, and as decorative elements engraved on bowls and vases fashioned from colourful stones and crystals. Popular materials of a durable nature were agate, chalcedony, sardonyx, rock crystal and jasper. Softer minerals skillfully worked were garnet, haematite, lapis-lazuli, malachite and travertine marbles. Gemstones were cut in various shapes including round and oval cabochons and many with flattened reflective surfaces inspired by natural crystal faces. Sometimes the crystals themselves were embellished and elaborated with random facets.

During the Renaissance, cameos, intaglios and gemstone carvings reached high levels of creative and technical excellence, cut by artists, sculptors and jewellers versatile in many of the fine arts. Delicately carved stone bowls and vases, mosaics and inlay work, were further tributes to lapidary skills. In Medieval Europe, superstition and belief in the supernatural lead to acquisition of amulets and talismanic jewellery cut from stones with special healing and magical attributes. That this conception has persisted through the centuries to the present time is shown by the interest in lucky charms and birth-stones.

Stones cut for jewellery changed in style with the advance of cutting techniques and recognized forms of facet cuts emerged. In later centuries lapidary arts continued to flourish with increased demands for jewellery to complement flamboyancy in dress and personal adornment. As a result of the insatiable vogue for collecting cut stones as works of art and for their antique value,

Figure 2. Jewellers drilling and polishing beads. Fragment of a wall panel. Egyptian XVIIIth Dynasty (courtesy of the Trustees, British Museum, London)

Figure 3. Amber chess set. Carved amber chess pieces and board of amber inlays. Blair Castle, Scotland (courtesy of His Grace, the Duke of Atholl)

large collections were passed on from generation to generation and are now housed in private galleries and museums throughout the world.

One can marvel at the skill and patience of the craftsman cutting into the hardest minerals with limited tools and materials, for example a wall-panel fragment in the British Museum, London, (figure 2) shows Egyptian lapidaries drilling beads by frictional movement of sticks between the hands and turning with strings on a bow-drill principle. The points of the stick drills would be fed with abrasive sands in a well of clay. In many parts of the world native lapidaries still cut and polish stones on primitive equipment using the traditional methods of their ancestors.

Tools used by early lapidaries for engraving and carving included sharp fragments of quartz, ruby, sapphire and splintered diamond set in wood and metal holders. Bow-saws and sand drills were used in slicing and piercing, while shaping was done on

5

Figure 4. Ornamental clock decorated with polished gemstones, reputed to be connected with Cardinal Richelieu. Blair Castle, Scotland (courtesy of His Grace, the Duke of Atholl)

Figure 5. Relief carving in jet, representing King Oswy and his Queen. Whitby Museum, Yorkshire, England (courtesy of Whitby Literary and Philosophical Society)

rubbing blocks and wheels of coarse stone. For smoothing and refinements leather pads, sticks and discs of metal, stone and hard wood were employed in conjunction with abrasive pastes. These were made from crushed pumice, sand and powdered corundum or emery mixed with water and oils. Pastes of haematite, metallic oxides, clays and other earthy substances, charcoal and powdered wood ash, were among materials used for polishing. It is highly probable that the value of metallic oxides as a polishing media was fully explored by early Egyptian lapidaries as these were already being used as pottery glazes; for example, white glaze was made from tin, yellow from silver, blues and greens from copper, black, reds and browns from manganese and haematite.

During the 19th and early 20th centuries in Britain, lapidaries exploited local mineral deposits and many small craft industries were producing objects made from serpentines, marbles and

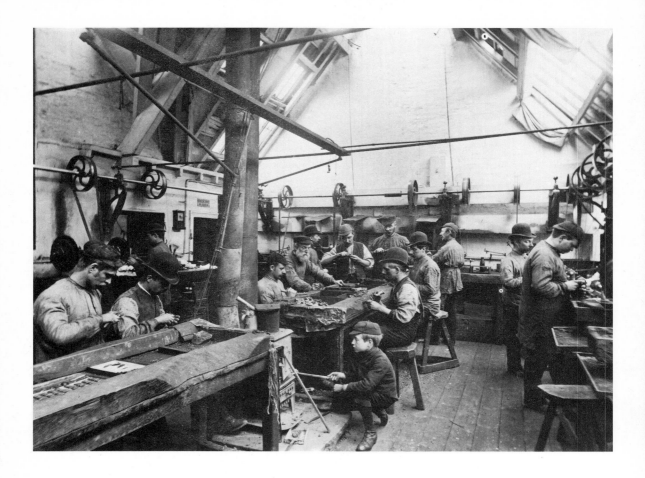

Figure 6. Jet carvers' workshop, Whitby, England. From an early photograph by Frank Meadow Sutcliffe (reproduced by permission of W. Eglon Shaw)

alabaster. In particular, Whitby jet carvings and Blue John (fluorite) ornaments are now prized as collector's items.

Now lapidary has become an almost universal leisure craft practised by people in all age groups and may well be regarded in the future as a popular folk art distinct from commercial and professional cutting. Educational values of the craft are being explored in schools and a rapid growth of lapidary societies has been noted in recent years. It is interesting to find that amateur lapidaries are attempting every known aspect of this ancient craft from the exacting geometry of facetting stones to creative skills of cameo cutting, carving and inlay work. Much of the work has been simplified by the production of machines and abrasives for every process and with the facilities now available there is no reason why the amateur lapidary should not create works of art equal to those of the craftsman of the past.

2 Choice of Stones

As there are many books on rocks and minerals available for specialized study the scientific and technical data on these subjects has been simplified in this chapter to provide background information relevant to practical lapidary work. For those wanting a more detailed knowledge of the many aspects of mineralogy and crystalography a list of such books is appended.

Stones for lapidary use must be of a composition suitable to withstand the effects of prolonged abrasion during shaping and also providing durable surfaces for polishing. Both hard and soft stones will cut and polish but some are structurally unsuitable with lack of cohesion in surface particles preventing formation of a uniform glaze. Those composed of several minerals may produce mixed qualities of finish due to undercutting of the softer portions.

Since all lapidary processes involve shaping by means of scratching and abrading the surfaces of stones, hardness or degree of resistance to abrasion is important to the cutter. Hardness of rocks and minerals is governed by the arrangement of structural atoms tightly or loosely bonded within the component forms. Scales of hardness have been devised to assist with identification and classification of mineral groups and the simplest of these, Mohs' scale, is based on the ability of a mineral to scratch another of softer composition occupying a position lower down the scale. Minerals are listed from one to ten with talc the softest mineral and diamond the hardest, but such an arbitrary guide gives little indication of the proportionate range of hardness between the listed minerals. A comparatively more accurate assessment is shown in the Knoop scale which is formulated on a diamond indentation system. Any such scales will show variations as the hardness value can only strictly be applied to the particular piece of material being tested and differences can occur in the same group of minerals. A comparison of Mohs' and Knoop scales is as follows

	Mohs' Scale	Approximate Knoop values
Talc	1	Not given
Gypsum	2	61
Calcite	3	141
Fluorite	4	181
Apatite	5	483
Orthoclase	6	621
Quartz	7	788
Topaz	8	1190
Corundum	9	2200
Diamond	10	8000

This clearly shows that the difference in hardness between corundum and diamond is far greater than between corundum and the softest mineral.

Relative hardness of abrasives

Based on Mohs' scale		Approximate Knoop rating
Aluminium oxide	8–9	2000
Silicon carbide	9–10	2480
Boron carbide	9–10	2760
Diamond	10	8000

Other physical properties important to the lapidary are *cleavage* and *fracture*. When a mineral splits along structural planes of weakness parallel to possible crystal faces this is referred to as cleavage and is categorized as perfect, distinct or good, imperfect or poor, depending on the ease with which it can be split. Crystals can have multiple planes of cleavage, for example parallel to octahedral faces as in diamond and fluorite, or a single plane as in topaz with perfect basal cleavage, but quartz and beryl have no cleavage planes. When cutting material which cleaves easily the table facet should be oriented 5 to 15 degrees out of parallel to a cleavage plane. Complications may arise for the cutter with crystals having twinned growth producing a false cleavage or parting when subjected to excess pressure or overheating.

In addition to natural cleavage some minerals break or splinter in different ways, forming distinctive fracture surfaces described in such terms as conchoidal (shell-like), splintery or fibrous, hackly or uneven. In many cases these fracture surfaces are useful in identifying a rough gem crystal.

Faceted stones are usually cut from transparent crystals in the upper hardness range and possessing special optical properties which are fully revealed when correctly cut in suitable styles. Refracted light rays entering the stone are dispersed into spectrum components and reflected back from the rear facets in sparkling colour or 'fire'. Degrees of refraction and internal reflection of light are measureable and are classified in tables of refractive indices for different minerals. Stones with a high refractive index and high dispersion properties will produce the greatest brilliancy when correctly cut. Some crystals are doubly refractive, producing duplicity of images by dividing the incident light ray and this can be seen in doubling of the back facets in cut stones of zircon and peridot.

The density or specific gravity of minerals is important to the gemmologist for identification and can be tested by immersing a crystal or cut stone in a heavy liquid of known density. By adding suitable diluents the specific gravity of the stone can be calculated when it remains suspended in the fluid. As some of these solutions are poisonous they must be used with caution.

For general lapidary work, ornamental and decorative stones in hardness equivalents of 1 to 7 (Mohs' scale) are used in a variety of processes. Materials can be opaque to transparent and selected for surface appearance, for example colour and pattern, or vibrant qualities of light reflected from internal structure and inclusions. Effects produced in this way, enhanced when cut as cabochons, are said to be *chatoyant* (cats-eye stones) or have *schiller,* (a translucent glow of light on lamellar planes, as in moonstone), and *opalescence* (an iridescent play of light and colour when viewed from different angles). Some minerals also have a characteristic lustre, expressed in such terms as metallic, waxy, pearly, vitreous, silky and adamantine, which is evident on both polished and freshly broken surfaces.

Where to obtain stones for polishing

Many lapidaries and collectors obtain their own materials on field excursions to recognized sites yielding rocks of common distribution and the more exotic, rare minerals. In many parts of the world natural deposits of ornamental and gemstone minerals can be collected in the field, notably Australia, New Zealand, Canada and USA, but in Britain only a limited amount of cutting material is found.

Rocks and minerals for lapidary use have worldwide distribution through dealers and retail suppliers. Personal visits to lapidary supply centres are generally welcomed and buyers are encouraged to browse through selections of graded rough, but a large volume of orders are dealt with by post. Dependent on type and quality, cutting material is sold by the pound, ounce or carat and here it should be stressed that for best results and economical use the more expensive material of good quality should be purchased.

For general use (tumbling or cutting cabochons) material can be bought in large pieces or broken down to workable sizes but rocks can be obtained ready sliced (slabbed) at extra cost if desired. Although transportation and handling are made easier by reducing the size of rocks, hammering or crushing methods can result in fractured material and this is not always apparent. Rough stones should be examined carefully by holding against a good light or by wetting the surface.

Flawless areas in crystals of facetting quality are seldom large, restricting many cut stones to small dimensions. Because of this the usable portions must be isolated with care to prevent waste, making further allowances for possible orientation. Flaws can often be easily detected in minerals retaining natural crystal faces or by polishing a small area to permit internal inspection against a strong light. Alternatively, the crystal can be placed in a glass containing a clear fluid of similar refractive index to the stone. The edges of transparent crystals will lose their clarity but internal fractures will interrupt the passage of light, spreading the light rays, and reveal the presence of imperfections.

Coloured crystalline rough should have uniform distribution of colour as any variation of hue will upset the optical symmetry of the cut stone. Mixed colouration or changes in colour intensity should not be confused with colour zoning.

Synthetic gemstone rough suitable for facetting possesses many of the characteristics of natural stones of the same chemical structure. Differences between the two can be determined by carrying out a series of gemmological tests and during cutting allowances may have to be made for a higher refractive index when calculating facet angles.

In the following list of stones suitable for cutting an abbreviated coding will indicate which can be used for more than one process, i.e. cabs (cabochons), tu (tumbling), cam (cameos), int (intaglio), car (carving). Additional abbreviations: R.I. (Refractive index), H. (Hardness – Mohs' scale).

STONES SUITABLE FOR CUTTING

AGATE VARIETIES *Cryptocrystalline quartz*	H.7, Heat sensitive cabs, tu. car.
Banded, fortification, orbicular	White to pale blue chalcedony with red, brown, black, yellow or green banding or circular patterns
Moss agate	Clear translucent chalcedony with green, red or blue moss–like inclusions
Dendritic or tree agate	White to pale brown, opaque. Dendritic inclusions of bright green, brown or black resembling branches of tree growth
Plume and flame agate	Translucent. Fused colouration suggesting feathers or smoke and flames
Scenic agate	Opaque – translucent. Inclusions suggest landscape features
Lace agate	Opaque – translucent. Finely banded in intricate lacy patterns
ALABASTER *Finely deposited gypsum*	H.2 Translucent. car. White to pink
AMAZONITE *Microcline feldspar*	H.6, cabs. tu. car. Pale to medium turquoise green. Schiller effect when correctly orientated

AMBER *Organic – fossilised resin*	H.2½, cabs. car. Lemon-yellow to orange-brown, red. Sometimes contains insects or fragments of vegetation
AVENTURINE *Crystalline quartz*	H.7, cabs. tu. Light to deep green, blue. Translucent. Contains silvery flecks of mica

CHALCEDONY VARIETIES *Cryptocrystalline quartz*

Bloodstone	H.6½–7, cabs. tu. car. int. cam. Opaque. Dark Green spotted with red. Brittle
Chalcedony	Milky white to pale blue
Carnelian	Translucent. Orange to red
Chrysoprase	Translucent. Bright green
Jasper	Opaque. Chalcedony fused with coloured oxides. Red, green, yellow to brown
Onyx	Layered white, black and grey. Traditional cameo material
Sard	Opaque. Red-brown
Sardonyx	Layered red-brown and white
HAEMATITE *Iron Oxide*	H.5½–6, cabs. int. Sometimes cut with facets. Black with metallic lustre
HOWLITE *Calcium boro-silicate*	H.3, cabs. car. Opaque. White, white veined with black
IVORY *Organic*	H.2½, car. White, creamy white. Tough, compact and durable. Good for detailed carving

JADE

Nephrite	H.6–6½, Cabs. tu. car. White to dark green. Tough, compact material often used for carving
Jadeite	H.6½–7, cabs. tu. car. Green to blue-green, brown red, mauve. Also tough and compact. Used for carving
JET *Organic – fossil wood*	H.2½–3½, cabs. car. Intense black. Compact, but easily worked. Takes a high polish

LABRADORITE *Plagioclase feldspar*	H.6, cabs. Dark blue. Displays spectrum colours when viewed in different positions due to lamellar twinning
LAPIS LAZULI *Lazurite*	H.5–5½, cabs. car. Opaque. Ultramarine blue flecked with iron pyrite. Inferior quality streaked with grey and white calcite
MALACHITE *Copper carbonate*	H.3–4, cabs. car. Opaque. Deep to pale green. Ribbon and orbicular banding
MOONSTONE *Orthoclase feldspar*	H.6–6½, cabs. Translucent. Clear to blue. Displays moving band of light on surface
OBSIDIAN *Volcanic glass*	H.5, cabs. tu. car. Opaque – translucent. Intense black to mahogany brown. Colour can be evenly distributed or striped, smoky with rainbow sheen. Starlike inclusions of white or grey known as snowflake obsidian. Smoky brown nodules known as 'Apache tears'. Brittle
OPAL *Hydrated silica*	H.5½–6½, cabs. car. Amorphous. Precious opal shows play of spectrum colours, varying in intensity. Heat sensitive and brittle
PETRIFIED WOOD *many varieties*	Mineral replacement of wood by agate, jasper or opal. Hardness according to composition. cabs. tu. car.
QUARTZ *Crystalline varieties*	H.7, cabs. tu. car. int.
Rock crystal	Colourless, water-clear. Transparent
Rose quartz	Translucent, Pale pink
Amethyst	Transparent to translucent. Purple, sometimes with colour zoning or white bands.
Citrine	Transparent. Pale to deep yellow

Smoky quartz	Transparent. Light to dark brown
RHODOCHROSITE *Manganese carbonate*	H.4, cabs. car. Opaque – translucent. Pale pink to red with white. Satin sheen
RHODONITE *Manganese silicate*	H.5–6, cabs. tu. car. Opaque. Pale pink to deep red, veined with black or yellow. Tough
RUTILATED QUARTZ *Crystalline quartz*	H.7, cabs. tu. Transparent with inclusions of golden rutile needles. Colourless or smoky brown
SERPENTINE *many varieties*	H.2$\frac{1}{2}$–4, cabs. car.
Chrysotile	White, greenish. Fibrous
Verde Antique	Dark green and white mottled. Opaque
Bowenite	Light green, translucent
Precious serpentine	Yellow-green, translucent. Often given locality names such as Iona Marble and Connemara Marble, etc
Massive serpentine	Dark green, red mottled. Opaque
SOAPSTONE *Talc*	H.1–1$\frac{1}{2}$, car. Opaque. Green, grey-green, mottled. Also known as steatite
SODALITE *Sodium aluminium silicate*	H.5$\frac{1}{2}$–6, cabs. tu. car. Opaque. Light to deep blue streaked with white or grey
TIGER'S EYE (Crocidolite) *Silicified asbestos*	H.7, cabs. tu. car. Opaque. Golden yellow to brown, blue to green. If heat treated – red. Silky fibres give chatoyance
TRAVERTINE ONYX (Banded calcite)	H.3, car. Translucent. Many pale Colours – white, yellow, green, brown
TOURMALINE IN QUARTZ *Crystalline quartz*	H.7, cabs. tu. Transparent, with needle-like inclusions of black tourmaline

VARISCITE *Aluminium phosphate*	H.4½, cabs. Opaque. Light green to blue-green. Vitreous lustre

This is by no means an exhaustive list of stones for cutting. Many types of marble and fossil limestones have been carved and the Blue John variety of fluorite turned as bowls and vases. Different kinds of material becomes available as lapidary dealers continually import stones from many parts of the world.

GEM MINERALS TO FACET

ANDALUSITE H.7½, R.I. 1·62–1·64	Green, red-brown. Cleavage: poor
APATITE H.5, R.I. 1·64	Green, yellow, blue colourless. Brittle. Heat sensitive
BERYL VARIETIES H.7½–8, R.I. 1·57–1·59	Emerald – deep green. Aquamarine – blue to green. Morganite – salmon pink. Cleavage – none
CHRYSOBERYL H.8½, R.I. 1·74–1·75	Alexandrite – red-green shows colour change, green in daylight – red in artificial light
CORUNDUM H.9, R.I. 1·76–1·77	Ruby – deep red. Sapphire – pale to deep blue. Cleavage: none
DIOPTASE H.5, R.I. 1·64–1·70	Deep green. Cleavage: good
EPIDOTE H.6½, R.I. 1·72–1·78	Yellow, green, brown. Cleavage: perfect
FLUORITE H.4, R.I. 1·43	Colourless, yellow, green, blue, purple. Cleavage: perfect in four directions

GARNET VARIETIES

Grossular H.6½–7, R.I. 1·77–1·81	Green, red, brownish/orange
Pyrope H.7½, R.I. 1·75–1·77	Red
Almandine H.7½, R.I. 1·78–1·83	Red, brown
Spessartite H.7½, R.I. 1·79–1·82	red, orange
Demantoid H.6½–7, R.I. 1·78–1·83	Green-yellow
KYANITE H.5–7, R.I. 1·71–1·73	Blue, Hardness change with directional orientation. Cleavage: perfect

PERIDOT H. 6½–7 R.I. 1·67	Yellow, green, brown. Not heat sensitive
PREHNITE H.6–6½, R.I. 1·61–1·64	Light green, translucent. Cleavage: distinct
QUARTZ VARIETIES H.7, R.I. 1·55	Rock crystal – colourless. Amethyst – purple. Smoky (Cairngorm) – brown. Citrine – yellow. Cleavage: none
SPODUMENE VARIETIES H.6½–7, R.I. 1·66–1·67	Kunzite – lilac. Hiddenite – yellow. Cleavage: perfect
TOPAZ H.8, R.I. 1·61–1·63	Colourless, blue, pink, pale green, yellow, brown. Not heat sensitive. Cleavage: perfect
TOURMALINE H.7–7½, R.I. 1·62–1·64	Deep green, red, blue, pink, black. Cleavage: none
ZIRCON H.7–7½, R.I. 1·78–1·98	Colourless, blue, green, yellow, brown, red. Brittle

Many other transparent crystalline minerals could be added to the list but some are extremely rare and others are too soft to be considered as gems but are of interest to the collector of faceted stones.

SYNTHETIC GEM CRYSTALS

CORUNDUM H.9, R.I. 1·76	Synthetic ruby and sapphire. Also in colours simulating danburite, rose topaz, tourmaline, alexandrite, etc
CHATHAM EMERALD H.7½, R.I. 1·56	Deep green
RUTILE (Titania) H.6½–7, R.I. 2·62	Colourless. High dispersion
SPINEL H.8, R.I. 1·72	Wide range of colours, simulating aquamarine, peridot, tourmaline, red spinel and zircon
STRONTIUM TITANATE H.5½–6, R.I. 2·41	Colourless, with no natural counterpart
YTTRIUM ALUMINIUM GARNET (YAG) H.7½, R.I. 1·83	Colourless, red, green. No natural counterpart

3 Abrasives and polishes

Abrasives used for gem-cutting must have the ability to penetrate and scratch the surfaces of stones for gradual stock removal. This is only possible where the abrasive is harder than the gem mineral and variations in the hardness of stones will determine both the rate of cutting and choice of abrasive. Coarse abrasion removes the bulk of material to produce the desired gem shape followed by systematic smoothing using finer abrasive grains. Subsequent scratches become so minute they are no longer visible to the naked eye.

Abrasive materials manufactured from silicon carbide and diamond are among the more versatile and widely used products available to the lapidary. Boron carbide, used as an industrial abrasive, is harder than silicon carbide but has less effective cutting power for sustained use on gem minerals. This is partially due to differences in the crystalline structure and sharpness of fracture in the abrasive grains. Research now being conducted into the use of boron carbide for lapidary purposes may soon provide a whole new range of cutting products.

Silicon carbide is a synthetic mineral used as loose abrasive grains and also forms the cutting ingredient of grinding wheels and coated abrasives of many types. Extreme hardness and rapid cutting qualities of the sharp crystalline grains make this an important abrasive medium. The main constituents in the production of silicon carbide are silica in the form of glass sand, and carbon (petroleum coke), and to these are added sawdust and salt. The mixture is placed in a furnace and electrically fired to high tem-

Figure 7. Silicon carbide crystals manufactured by the Carborundum Company Ltd

peratures, resulting in a fused mass of sharp iridescent crystals (figure 7) which are later crushed and refined into classified grain sizes. Crushed grain particles are sifted through screens of different mesh sizes to obtain a range of graded grits. The grade numbers, such as 60, 80, 100 etc, are determined by the size of the grits passing through screens having a specific number of openings to the linear inch. For example, 60 grit will have been sifted through a mesh with 60 openings to the inch. Above grain sizes of 200 grit cohesion makes screening difficult and the very finest particles are classed as powders or flours. These are sized, among other methods, through a sedimentation or wet grading process measured by the settling rate of particles in water.

GRINDING WHEELS

For general lapidary use silicon carbide grinding wheels are employed for basic grinding and shaping of gem material. Information giving instant recognition of a wheel's characteristics and suitability for the purpose is contained in a series of symbols printed on an absorbent disc label on the side of the wheel. The labels should remain in position for as long as possible during use. Distribution of symbols may vary between manufacturers but a typical example of label marking is shown in figure 8. The abrasive

Figure 8. Silicon carbide grinding wheel with label marking identifying the wheel's characteristics

silicon carbide will be denoted by a letter 'C' followed by a numbered grit size. A purer form of silicon carbide, giving the wheel a green colour, will show letters 'GC' (green grit silicon carbide). Wheel hardness, letters A–Z, is governed by ratios of bonding material and abrasive grains which combine to resist wear and grinding stress. A structure number refers to grain spacing, dense or open, and the lower numbers indicate a structure of extreme density. The type of bond recommended by manufacturers for lapidary wheels is vitrified and is denoted by the letter 'V' (figure 9). A vitrified bond consists of clay bodies and other ceramic minerals such as feldspar and silica mixed with graded abrasive particles. The mixture is moulded and pressed into required wheel dimensions and fired in a kiln to vitrify the bond. The vitreous matrix is tough enough to support the abrasive grits during cutting but is sufficiently brittle to allow the release of blunt particles when subjected to increased stress.

The bond and structure of wheels is very important and it is generally accepted that hard stones cut more rapidly on softer bonded wheels of open grain structure, and that softer stones can be ground more efficiently on hard–bonded wheels of close

Figure 9. Grinding wheel symbols

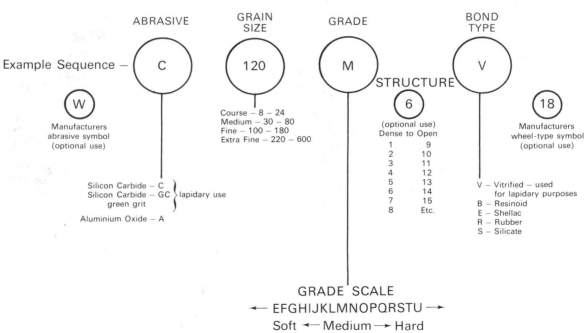

GRINDING WHEEL SYMBOLS
Based on British Standardized Marking System

structure. A hard grinding wheel makes little impression on a hard stone and tends to glaze on the peripheral cutting face, causing the stone to slide over the surface. Wheels with softer bonding allow worn abrasive grains to be released, exposing new cutting edges as grinding proceeds. As a result, softer wheels wear down more rapidly when cutting a succession of hard minerals. Open-grained structures allow water used during grinding to penetrate deeper into the cutting surface to cool grit particles. This is important to counteract the effects of frictional heat generated by hard abrasion. Clogging of the wheel's surface is also lessened by a more efficient flushing action of the coolant as it removes grinding waste from the open structure. The build-up of waste, however, is less evident when cutting hard stones and can be controlled by the grit size of the wheel. Accumulation of sludge and waste material during cutting is more pronounced with softer stones but is more readily washed away from tightly bonded grit particles of a harder wheel.

COATED ABRASIVES

Surface coated abrasive discs and belts are used for sanding or refining following grinding. Progressively finer grades of abrasives remove marks from previous stages to prepare the stone for polishing. Modern abrasives used for surface coating in industrial finishing processes are aluminium oxide and silicon carbide, both electric furnace products. For lapidary work silicon carbide is the more efficient general purpose abrasive and coated discs are manufactured to various requirements. Backing materials for belts and discs can be of natural or synthetic fabric and paper, and are made in degrees of flexibility. Distribution of the surface grits or abrasive particles is close or open and these are bonded to the backing with various glues, varnishes or resins. Open grit distribution permits flushing of deposits from softer minerals which tend to overload the sanding surface. As water coolant is generally used during sanding, the type of bond selected must be suitable for retention of grits and water-soluble glues, for example, would be unsatisfactory in this situation.

LOOSE ABRASIVE GRITS

Silicon carbide grits in loose powder form are used by the lapidary for a number of techniques, notably in conjunction with horizontal metal laps for smoothing flat rock sections prior to polishing and can be used for facetting softer minerals. Loose abrasives can also serve a similar function to coated discs for sanding shaped stones following grinding stages. Stones processed by tumbling methods are ground and refined by progressively finer abrasive powders.

Diamond abrasives

Natural and synthetic diamond is the hardest substance available to the lapidary and as an abrasive is capable of cutting all known gem minerals. Crushed diamond particles are carefully graded through numbered mesh screens and also further reduced to finer micron sized powders. The following data shows the relationship between screen and particle sizes.

Micron Size	Grit Mesh Size
1	14000
3	8000
6	3000
15	1200
30	600
45	325

Diamond particles are processed for many lapidary uses and effectively bonded to appropriate cutting tools and surfaces. Bonding may be formed by pressure impregnation into soft metals, often carried out by the gem-cutter, or by manufacturing processes such as electroplating and sintering. Sintering is a method where powdered metal and compacting fillers are combined with diamond particles and pressed into a firm mass, to be finally sintered and bonded to metal cutting surfaces such as saw blades and drills where maximum rigidity and abrasive durability is required. Dry diamond powders, compounds and pastes are also produced for numerous applications and used in conjunction with a wide range of grinding and polishing supports.

DIAMOND SAW BLADES

Saw blades of this type consist of thin circular discs of metal with diamond particles bonded to the rim to form a continuous cutting edge. Unlike saws used for woodworking which have metal serrations to rip through the wood grain, diamond saws have no teeth and cut through the rock by a gradual process of abrasion. Two main types are manufactured for lapidary use; the notched-rim blade with diamonds sealed in regularly spaced slits in the periphery, and the sintered-rim type with a surface bonding of diamond and powdered metal (see figure 10). Saw blades are used with an adequate supply of coolant and lubricant to maintain maximum blade life and efficiency.

DIAMOND DRILLS

Surface plated and sintered drill bits are the two main types in general use and these are made in various diameter sizes to fit

Figure 10. Types of diamond saw blades: (a) notched rim (b) continuous sintered rim (c) segmented sintered rim

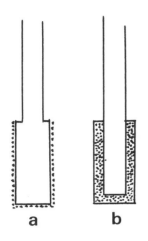

Figure 11. Diamond drill tips (a) electro-plated single layer (b) sinter tip

the securing chuck of drills which range from small battery-operated hand tools to larger power drills. While electroplating deposits a single veneer of metal–bonded diamond on the drill tip, sintered drills have a mixture of metal and diamond powder fused to the drill bit and this provides a greater depth of diamond (figure 11). As the drills usually revolve at high speeds, continuous coolant fluids are essential to prevent overheating and also to provide a flushing action at point of contact.

DIAMOND WHEELS

Metal diamond wheels with the peripheral face plated or sintered with diamond particles perform a similar function to other types of grinding wheels for shaping and smoothing stones but are not as widely used by the amateur gem-cutter. Although more expensive to produce, the diamond wheels combine durability with faster cutting and overheating is minimized (figure 12).

Figure 12. Diamond grinding wheel. Manufactured by Diamond Pacific Tool Corporation, Barstow, California.

For general use, present-day diamond laps are usually made of copper impregnated with diamond particles over the working surface and are manufactured in graded grit sizes. Other metal laps can serve a similar purpose and are frequently charged with diamond powders by the lapidary to suit particular requirements. Diamond pastes are also applied to a variety of surfaces and lap shapes such as grooved and cup-shaped hard wood, moulded plastic and the more orthodox flat metal types.

Polishes

Polishing is the final stage of a series of refining processes and results in a flawless, highly reflective surface. Materials used for this purpose include various mineral oxides such as tin oxide, aluminium oxide, cerium oxide, zirconium oxide and chrome oxide. Of these, cerium and tin oxides have proved to be the most popular general purpose polishing media for a variety of gem minerals.

Diamond pastes and powders in the finer micron range are also used in conjunction with suitable supports to produce a final polish. Diamond compounds supplied in syringe applicators and used with appropriate extending fluid continues the abrasive process and, by removal of remaining surface scratches, imparts a high gloss finish to the gems. The abrasive action of the oxide polishes is less pronounced and the combination of a powdered oxide, used as a water-based slurry, and the resistant buffing surface can create sufficient heat to produce a glazing of the stone's surface in many cases. This is known as the Bielby layer and is partly due to the melting and flow of surface molecules in the gem structure, followed by recrystallization upon cooling. During polishing excessive frictional heat can sometimes result in uneven surfaces due to shifting and re-deposition of the cooling structure flowing over unpolished, roughened portions of the stone.

Polishing agents in general use are:

Cerium oxide	One of a group of substances known as rare earth minerals. Powder form, yellow to pale orange
Tin oxide	Powdered oxide of tin. Creamy white.
Zirconium oxide	White powder obtained from the mineral zircon
Aluminium oxide	Corundum. Very hard crystalline structure. Obtained as fine white powder
Chrome oxide	Chromium mineral. Oxide produced as deep green powder

4 Machinery

Any decision on equipment will involve the question of expenditure but, where workshop facilities and skills permit, machines and accessories can be made from standard fittings and materials obtainable from hardware stores with considerable saving in costs. Also, many lapidary dealers stock machine parts for assembly in the home workshop on a unit construction basis. Comparison of costs for machines and sundries can be obtained from a selection of lapidary dealers' catalogues and studying the manufacturers' specifications will give an indication of requirements for particular needs. Before making final commitments, discussion with people having similar interests or members of local lapidary clubs will prove helpful when choosing equipment, but inevitably there will be slight variance of opinion due to personal preferences. Information is also available from education or community centres offering lapidary courses. Technical handbooks on many aspects of lapidary have been published in recent years, adding to sources of reference, and periodicals devoted exclusively to the subject supply expert guidance and vital links between readers and suppliers.

The range of lapidary equipment is wide and the most suitable choice for individual needs presents many problems which are discussed more fully in the next chapter, but the following information will enable the complete beginner to understand the basic construction of various types of machines and the processes for which they are designed. The appropriate operating speeds are given in Table 4.

Types of equipment

DIAMOND SAWS

Rock sections or slices are cut on machines operating diamond saw blades mounted, as a general rule, in either a vertical or horizontal position. The diameter of blades used for slabbing – a term used for slicing rock nodules or chunky gemstone rough – should be increased in proportion to the size of material to be slabbed. Small trim-saws with blade diameters below eight inches are used for lighter slitting tasks and trimming thin rock slices into workable pieces.

Basic components of a diamond saw incorporate a sturdy driving shaft to ensure maximum stability, with collars supporting the blade at least one third of the blade diameter and, in the case of a vertical saw, a flat saw bed and leakproof tank for coolant fluid. Adequate spray guards are essential and where possible the larger vertical slabbing saw should be entirely covered with a transparent canopy to contain coolant spray which is thrown off the

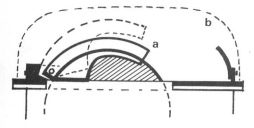

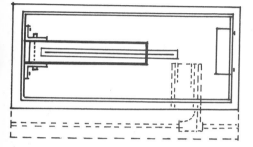

blade as a fine mist (figure 13). Separate saw units usually run at fixed speeds requiring a single shaft pulley but combination units operating a number of processes on the same shaft, either vertically or horizontally, should be fitted with a multiple pulley system linking shaft to motor to allow speed changes. Some form of rock clamp or vice is a standard feature on the larger saws and is essential on horizontal saws. In some cases there is a gravity feed or auto-matic feed device which gives an even rate of cutting to produce smooth rock slices. (Figures 14, 15, 16).

GRINDING AND POLISHING UNITS

Grinding stones into desired shapes is followed by *sanding* or smoothing to produce a refined surface ready for polishing. The silicon carbide grinding wheels, together with interchangeable abrasive discs and polishing attachment, are secured in position on a shaft revolving in either an upright or horizontal position. Machines are driven by a $\frac{1}{4}$ hp or 1/6 hp electric motor and a system of pulleys on shaft and motor, linked by a driving belt, provides speeds suited to each process. Water coolant is supplied to vertical grinding wheels from a controlled overhead drip-feed tank or from water contained in a shallow trough allowing the wheel periphery to skim the surface.

A combination unit incorporating trim-saw, grinding wheels and attachments for sanding and polishing will supply all the

Figure 13. Diamond saw. (a) adjustable guard on trim-saw (b) plastic canopy as spray shield fitted on slab saw (c) dotted lines show extended saw bed for slab saw to allow for rock clamp and guide rail

Figure 14. Highland Park 10-in. slabbing and trimming saw. Rock vice and carriage operated by gravity feed. Weighted tension cord (not shown) is attached to carriage and passed over small pulley on right of saw bed. Plastic spray cover removed. Highland Park Manufacturing Co. Inc., South Pasadena, California.

Figure 15. Kiwi 10-in. slabbing and trimming saw, manufactured in New Zealand. Rock vice and carriage propelled by automatic screw-feed. Plastic cover not shown

Figure 16. Evans TS1 6-in. trim saw. Hand operated screw-feed vice and carriage. Angled spray guard removed. Manufactured by H. C. Evans & Son, London, England

requirements for cutting cabochons. (Figures 17, 18, 19). Single grinding wheel units of this type usually require an alternative wheel change, followed by a succession of sanding discs. There are many design variations of extended lapidary units with two vertical grinders which allow uninterrupted progression through coarse and fine grinding stages. This not only saves time but allows more than one person to use the machine at once providing there is adequate spacing between the wheels (figure 20). Machines with drum sanders using coated abrasive sleeves of silicon carbide extend the range of equipment, and sanding on the front face of the drum follows the action of grinding in progressive sequence when cutting cabochons, thus retaining similarities of technique (figure 21). As an alternative, grooved wheels of hard wood or plastic for use with diamond compounds are favoured by many for cabochon sanding stages. These may be in multiples on a horizontal shaft (figures 22, 23), or form single grooved flat laps.

Where space is limited, a wide range of lapidary skills can be implemented on machines operating various attachments supported horizontally on a short vertical spindle (figure 24). Water and cutting debris are contained in a shallow bowl or tank. In addition to sawing and the usual sequences of cabochon cutting,

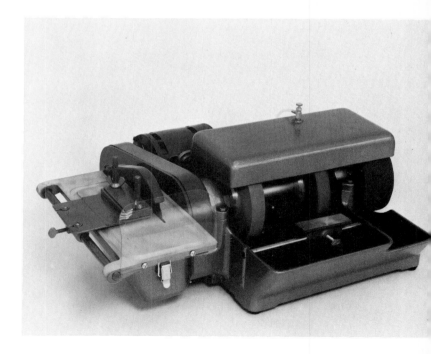

Figure 17. Highland Park 6-in. combination unit for sawing, grinding and polishing with drum sander on right. Overhead coolant supply. Saw table hinges back for access to blade and sump. Highland Park Manufacturing Co. Inc. South Pasadena, California

Figure 18. P.M.R.3. 8-in. combination unit for sawing grinding and polishing. Overhead coolant tank and control taps. P.M.R. Lapidary Supplies, Pitlochry, Scotland

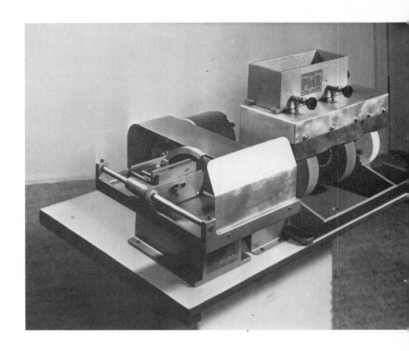

Figure 19. A versatile 6-in double grinder, sander, polisher unit, quickly converted to a trim saw combination machine by replacing one grinding wheel with a diamond blade and saw table. Manufactured by H. C. Evans & Son, London, England

Figure 20. Gemtek 6-in. double grinder, sanding and polishing unit fabricated in moulded glass-fibre. Water coolant supplied from trough below grinding wheels. Manufactured by Lapidary Wholesale Supplies, Hull, England

Figure 21. Star Diamond 8-in. grinder-polisher with drum sander on left. Water coolant piped to overhead control valves above wheels. Star Diamond Industries Inc., Harbor City, California

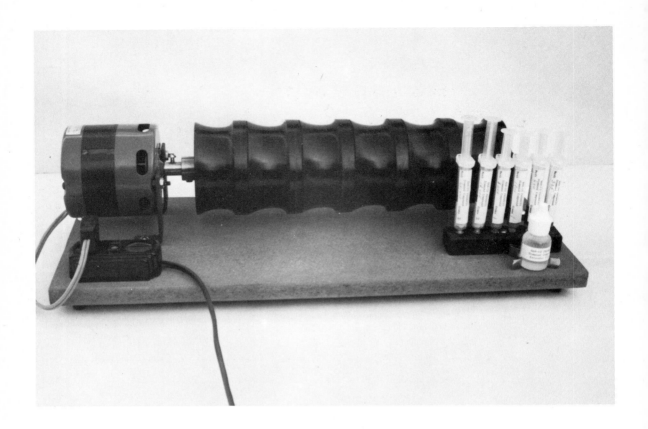

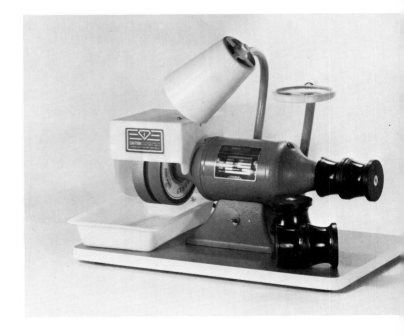

Figure 22. 'Gem-Pol' sander, polisher for diamond compounds. Laminated and tempered masonite rolls with direct drive from motor. Speed 1500 rev/mm. Diamond compound syringes and extender on right. Water coolant not used. Ran-co Products, Granada Hills, California

Figure 23. 'Genii', a self-contained all-diamond cabochon unit for grinding, sanding and polishing. Fitted with diamond wheels and rolls for diamond compounds. In rear, flexible-arm lamp and magnifier. Diamond Pacific Tool Corp., Barstow, California

Figure 24. Horizontal unit for sawing. grinding, sanding and polishing. Overhead coolant tank and pivotting rock clamp for sawing. Other attachments for this machine include vibrating lap and facetting head. Robilt Gemmaker, manufactured in Australia

attachments for simple facetting, also lapping flat sections by vibratory action, add to the versatility of machines of this type.

Cabochon units should have adequate wheel guards and an efficient method of supplying water to grinding wheels. This should be sufficiently well controlled to protect the user from water spray. Pulleys and belts must be guarded and electric motors should not be subject to flooding or splashing with water round the mountings. Shaft bearings play an important role in smooth running and efficiency and the permanently sealed type of bearings are preferable.

LAPS FOR FLAT SECTIONS

For processing flat sections such as sawn rock slabs or half nodules for display purposes a horizontal metal lap charged with silicon carbide grits provides a most effective method. Ideally laps should have a continuous surface uninterrupted by a central locking nut.

A felt or leather polishing disc replaces the metal lap for the final stage (figure 25).

Automatic lapping processes can be carried out on purpose–built vibratory machines or on special machine adaptations already mentioned. Rock slabs and abrasive particles are subjected to rapid vibration and lateral movement through high speed oscillation of the lap platform. Several slabs can be ground simultaneously by this method, followed by final polishing on a felt pad impregnated with suitable polishing agent (figure 26).

FACETTING UNITS

Accuracy in spacing and determining correctly angled facets on gemstones rests as much with the skill of the cutter as with mechanical sophistication. Elaborate machines can make the task easier but many simple devices are used to similar ends and these include various angled attachments as machine accessories (figure 27).

A basic facetting unit consists of a head assembly with a quadrant arc marked in degrees for correct facet angles and a dop arm which rotates for accurate placing of facets indicated by a locking index gear. Index gears are notched by numbered divisions which are usually divisible by eight – a number corresponding to

Figure 25. Gemtek Flat Lap. A flat lapping machine with cast iron lap in position for use with loose grits. Interchangeable with felt polishing lap. Manufactured by Lapidary Wholesale Supplies, Hull, England

36

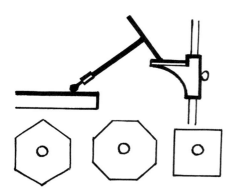

Figure 27. Dop attached to centre of angled templates used to index positions of symmetrical facets in simple cuts. Templates rest on an adjustable platform

the main facets on many types of cut. A cheater or index splitter is usually a standard feature on purpose-built equipment and is used to adjust the position of contact in a pre-indexed facet where required (figures 28, 29).

The whole facet head assembly can be raised or lowered on a stand rod supported rigidly on a substantial base which in the interests of stability should also house the shaft for the master lap. The stand rod can be moved backwards or forwards in a slot cut in the base. A circular metal plate known as the master lap acts as a support for the detachable cutting and polishing discs and is not in itself a lapping surface. A 1/6 hp motor is adequate and variable speeds can be obtained by using suitable pulley arrangements.

TUMBLE POLISHERS

Quantities of stones can be processed simultaneously by progressive phases of smoothing and polishing using simple methods of tumbling. There are two main categories of tumblers; rotary types with the load mass revolving within open or closed containers, and those with vibratory action causing rapid agitation of the stones inside fixed hoppers. Although processes and length of

Figure 28. Complete motorized facetting unit with assortment of metal dops and transfer block in foreground. Manufactured by A. and D. Hughes, Warley, Worcestershire

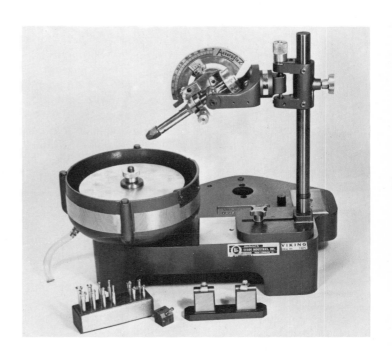

Figure 29. Viking Accura-flex. A complete facetting unit for precision cutting. Selection of metal dops, angle adaptor and transfer block also shown. Geode Industries Inc., New London, Iowa, USA.

tumbling time differ the end product in both instances is the same. Vibratory tumblers are most suitable where the time factor and a higher yield is important but for general lapidary use in the small workshop, revolving tumblers are manufactured in a range of sizes adequate for most requirements. The examples of tumblers shown will serve to illustrate some of the variations in design and construction of machines. (Figures 30, 31, 32). Although tumblers are stocked by some department stores and general craft shops it is better to buy from a recognized lapidary dealer who is able to give valuable advice.

FURTHER LAPIDARY AIDS

Drilling holes in stones and the removal of round section cores of material is done by specially manufactured drills and bits which are power operated. These range from large fixed bench drills to the hand-held battery-operated types.

Machines for cutting spheres are produced with interchangeable cups of different sizes and beadmaking mills are available for mass production of polished gemstone beads.

Figure 30. Robilt Tumbler (Australian) with round polythene barrels supported on two rollers. Belt driven from motor to large pulley for speed reduction

Figure 31. Highland Park KCB 10. A self-contained tumbler with angled barrel and detachable rubber liner to cushion the load

Care of equipment

Most lapidary machines are well constructed and designed for many years of service, particularly when correct usage and regular maintenance is observed. A few minutes spent in cleaning up a machine at the end of each working session is well worth the effort.

CARE OF DIAMOND SAWS

The saw must never be allowed to cut with insufficient coolant as this can cause severe overheating which may upset the balance of the metal disc and unseat the diamond particles. Accumulation of rock waste and gritty sludge in the tank should be removed frequently and replaced with clean oil or other coolant fluid.

Always keep the saw bed clear of grit and stone chips as any particles becoming wedged between blade and aperture in the

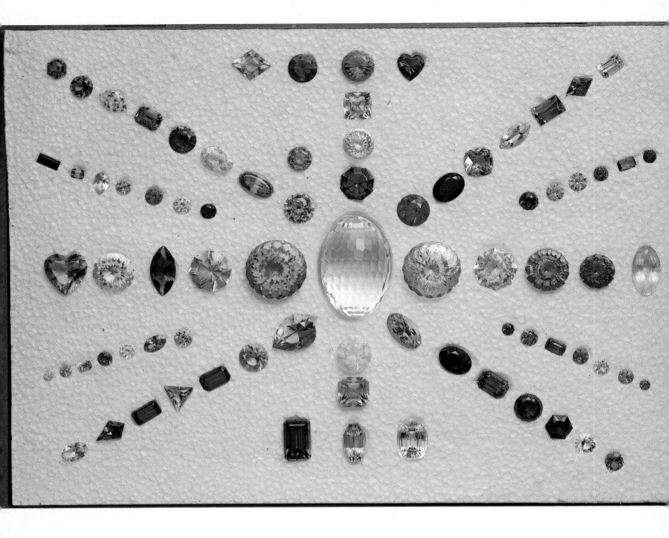

Plate 1. A collection of faceted gem-stones cut by Dennis Durham, Hull

Figure 32. Viking Vibra-sonic VT 35. A large capacity vibratory tumbler with vinyl-lined hopper. Geode Industries, New London, Iowa, USA

saw bed will wear into the side of the blade or may even damage the rim.

Some manufacturers recommend reversal of diamond blades periodically but some blades are designed to revolve in one direction only. These are usually marked with a directional arrow and should be mounted accordingly.

Diamond blades can be sharpened by clearing away burrs of metal which have been dragged over the diamond points by prolonged use on hard stones. Sharpening is done by sawing through a soft sand brick or similar material which allows gritty particles to roll over the metal and clean up the cutting points.

GRINDING WHEELS – HINTS ON USE AND MAINTENANCE

Maximum efficiency is obtained by selecting wheels of suitable bond and grit size for cutting stones at different stages i.e. coarse and fine grinding. Always grind on the front edge of the wheel, never on the side, and try to prevent a groove forming by using the whole cutting face. Severely grooved wheels can be dangerous when sharp flanges are formed. Excessive grinding pressure can damage both wheel and stone, and jabbing a pointed stone into a wheel can be equally disastrous. Bumping or 'chattering' of the wheel during cutting may be the result of grinding too large a stone or the wheel may be out of true. It is important to use the correct grinding speed; a wheel running too slowly will wear away quickly and make little impression on hard stones.

Adequate water coolant will prevent overheating and carry away sludge and loose particles during cutting, but the wheel must not be in contact with water when not in use. Moisture absorbed into a stationary wheel can weaken the bond in isolated places and present a further hazard. In such instances, do not use again until the wheel has dried out. This can be assisted by switching on the machine to spin off surplus moisture.

Wheel dressing

When the grinding face has become badly grooved or to liven up a new wheel which has a rather glazed surface, a wheel dressing tool of either the diamond tipped or wheel type should be used. A grinding wheel which has worn unevenly and is no longer perfectly round can also be corrected by use of a wheel dresser (figure 33).

Guards and workrests

Wheel guards on lapidary machines protect the user from coolant spray and stone particles should any splintering occur. Guards should overhang the wheel as far as possible without obstructing the operator's view, and any additional anti-splash attachments projecting below the end of the guards must not interfere with the smooth running of the wheel.

If machines are fitted with hand or work rests the clearance between rest and wheel periphery should not exceed 3 mm and any wheel dressing or wearing away during grinding will necessitate adjustment of the rest. Gaps between work rests and grinding wheels formed by deep grooving are a potential hazard and increase the risk of a stone or dopstick becoming wedged in the space.

Figure 33. Use of diamond point wheel dressers. (a) tool should be held at angle of 10–15 degrees pointing in downward direction (b) it is dangerous to allow space for dressing tool to slip between wheel and tool rest (c) diamond surfaced tool secured in clamp supported on tool rest. (d) single point dresser inclined at angle when traversing wheel face (e) single point dresser (f) multiple-point dresser used parallel to wheel face as shown in (c)

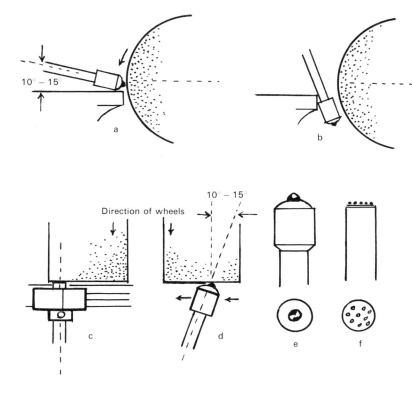

Mounting grinding wheels

In industry, standards for use and care of equipment are strictly governed by workshop regulations approved by factory inspectorate. This not only minimizes the risk of accidents but encourages a sound code of behaviour and observance of good workshop practice. Many lapidary clubs have evolved similar rules for the protection of members using lapidary machines incorporating grinding wheels. In industrial workshops the regulations for mounting abrasive wheels are regarded with such importance as to warrant the services of a skilled wheel fitter, specially trained and qualified for the task. In order to assist the lapidary who may be unfamiliar with standard grinding equipment the following points will be helpful when mounting straight-sided grinding wheels.

Ejection of fragments from a burst wheel is the main hazard; this rarely happens but can result from revolving at speeds in excess of the makers' instructions or faulty wheel mounting. Maximum permissible speeds are marked on a paper disc on the side of the wheel, and there the reader can be reassured since grinding speeds for lapidary purposes allow a very comfortable safety margin.

Prior to mounting, check the arbor size to ensure a close fit on the spindle. Test the wheel for soundness (vitrified wheels are brittle and damage may have occurred in transit) by suspending it in an upright position and tapping lightly with a non-metallic object. A good wheel will ring but be suspicious of a dull or deadened sound which may indicate a cracked wheel. Do not use.

The paper washers or blotters bearing essential data should be intact on both sides of the wheel. Diameters of the metal flanges supporting the wheel must be accurately matched to give uniform bearing surface and should not be less than one third of the wheel diameter. Flanges should have an inner recess to distribute the clamping pressure which must be clear of the centre hole and ordinary flat steel washers must not be used.

When securing the wheel in position do not use excessive force as this may crack it. Tightening the nut by hand pressure on a spanner is sufficient. Adjust the belt pulleys for correct speed and rotate the wheel by hand to ensure all-round clearance before switching on the power. As the machine starts, stand clear for a few revolutions as an extra safety precaution.

5 Equipping a Lapidary Workshop

Equipping a workshop for either individual or communal use will be largely influenced by economy, available working space and degrees of specialization which may embrace the simplest to the more exacting lapidary techniques. A lapidary workshop includes any situation where convenient spaces are utilized for the purpose, whether in the home, garden shed, school or clubroom, but whatever the circumstances the following important considerations should be taken into account.

Almost every lapidary process discussed throughout this book involves power-driven equipment of one kind or another; ranging from a hand tool for drilling and carving, to larger combination units for sawing and grinding. Motors of various sizes operate from normal domestic power circuits so machines should always be sited conveniently near to electrical sockets. Not only will this avoid the hazards of long, trailing leads, perhaps with intermediate junction boxes, but will also place the operator within easy reach of the main switch for emergencies.

Since water is used as a coolant in many cases, care must be taken to protect motors, switches, junction boxes from splashes and spray. Electricity must not be switched on or off with wet hands and a cloth or hand-towel placed near the machine will serve as a reminder. In all workshop situations good lighting is essential and where possible there should be concentrated light on the work.

The nuisance aspects of noise both to the lapidary and immediate neighbours may have a direct bearing on choice of lapidary processes and siting of equipment, which is clearly an individual problem. A certain amount of noise is unavoidable and this will increase or decrease in proportion to the scale of the machine. Other influencing factors such as smoothly running mechanical parts, a substantial work-bench and a rubber mat placed under the machine will help to minimize this problem. Noise produced by the swish and rattle of stones in tumbler barrels can be controlled to some extent by choice of barrel, for example rubberized containers or rubber liners will absorb some of the sound and this will be further reduced in tumblers of less capacity where load size is decreased proportionately.

Sawing with oily coolants can be a messy procedure and more suited to an outdoor workshop than a corner of the kitchen. Similarly, water and grinding dust may be undesirable in some indoor situations, limiting the use of standard grinding equipment in the home. In contrast, facetting and processes involving the use of diamond abrasives present few location problems and equipment can be used from any convenient electrical socket. Since diamond abrasives are clean to use, the need for precautions associated with grinding dust and abrasive slurries is eliminated.

In every type of workshop situation the need for adequate

Figure 34. A good example of a small lapidary workshop showing efficient organization and labelling of materials

storage space should not be overlooked. Loose grits should be kept in containers marked with the grit size and stored away from the polishing oxides. Laps should be placed in separate polythene bags, clearly labelled. Similar care to prevent contamination should be taken with diamond abrasives and laps (figure 34).

Expendable materials and miscellaneous equipment

It may be unnecessary to keep a supply of extra materials on hand in the individual workshop but where groups of people are using machines it is advisable to have spare grinding wheels and a diamond blade available as well as stocks of other expendable materials. Several miscellaneous items are also required to complete the equipment.

The following list may prove helpful when setting up a workshop or as a stock check for replacements and re-ordering supplies.

Many standard cabochon and lapping machines are fitted with basic accessories and any renewal of these should meet manufacturers specifications.

Spare diamond blade to fit saw.

Spare can of oil coolant for saw.

Spare silicon carbide grinding wheels, medium bond and structure, to fit arbor size of machine shaft. 120 and 220 grit.

Silicon carbide wet/dry sanding discs, belts or sleeves in 220, 400 and 600 grades.

Easy peel-off gum for fixing sanding discs to backing.

Squeezy bottles for water coolant.

Loose silicon carbide grits in several grades: 80, 120, 220, 320, 400, 600.

Small dishes and brushes to apply grit and water.

Polishing powders: cerium oxide, tin oxide and small amounts of chrome oxide and aluminium oxide.

Polythene bags to contain polishing laps.

Facilities for heating dopping wax eg. spirit lamp, gas flame or electrically heated dop plate.

Supply of dopping wax.

Dopping sticks (wooden dowel) of different diameters.

Plastic templates of various shapes and aluminium marker.

Diamond wheel dressing tool.

Tools such as spanners and screwdrivers.

Electrical items such as spare fuses, plugs adaptors, extension leads.

Bowls, jugs and buckets for water drainage from machines.

Liquid detergent for washing stones after sawing, or box containing degreasing granules.

Cleaning tissues, cotton waste or rags.

The home workshop

In the home restricted space may limit the hobby to tumbling as a means of polishing stones for jewellery and other decorative purposes. Tumblers should be selected according to needs, for it is important to remember that unlike methods where individual stones are cut to particular shapes and sizes the tumbling process produces large quantities of stones polished simultaneously and an accumulation of stones which may not be used is uneconomical.

As an introduction it may be sufficient to obtain a tumbler which operates small capacity barrels, permitting easy storage and minimum working space. Larger tumblers with single or multiple barrels yielding several pounds of polished stones are better suited to a space in a garage or workshed.

For those who wish to extend their lapidary skills to one of the more controlled forms of gemcutting the choice of machinery will again depend on the workshop space available. Many lapidaries would head the list of basic requirements with a diamond saw although this is not an essential item of equipment for the beginner. Slabbed rough (thin rock slices) can be purchased from dealers but it is an advantage to be able to trim slabs to size and slice small nodules and pebbles. This facility also saves considerable wastage which occurs through hammering or grinding stones into smaller pieces. Where space is limited perhaps the best solution would be to obtain a combination unit which includes a trim-saw, grinding wheel and detachable sanding/polishing discs in one machine.

Further choice of equipment ultimately depends on individual interests such as facetting or cutting cabochons for jewellery, preparation of flat sections as cabinet specimens or simply building up a collection of polished stones. Whatever specializations are envisaged, excellent small machines are obtainable for home use, with larger counterparts and accessories for more ambitious workshop projects.

Many amateur lapidaries obtain complete satisfaction and high degrees of competence with their own home-made equipment, and others, lacking motorized facilities, achieve good results using hand-polishing methods.

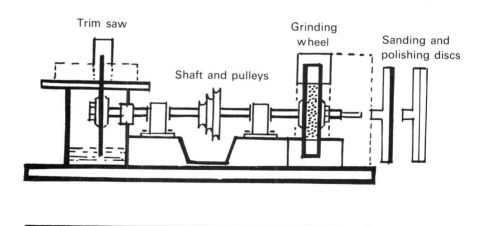

Figure 35. Diagram of a combination unit

Figure 36. Diagram of horizontal lapping and polishing machine

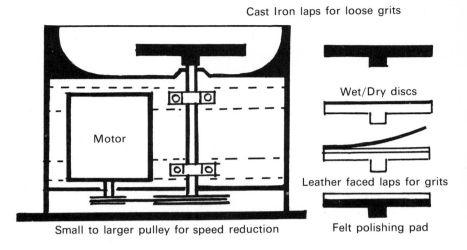

Cast Iron laps for loose grits

Wet/Dry discs

Leather faced laps for grits

Felt polishing pad

Motor

Small to larger pulley for speed reduction

Figure 37. Diagram of horizontal grinding, sanding and polishing unit

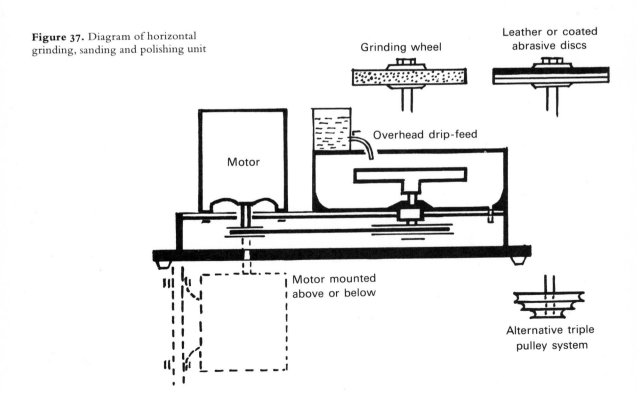

Grinding wheel

Leather or coated abrasive discs

Overhead drip-feed

Motor

Motor mounted above or below

Alternative triple pulley system

Figure 38. Diagram of double grinder, sander, polisher

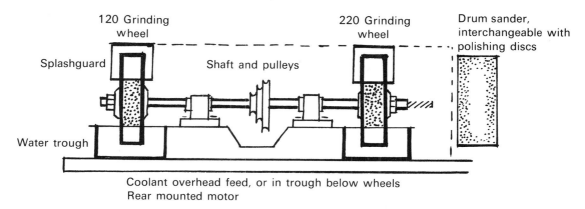

120 Grinding wheel

220 Grinding wheel

Drum sander, interchangeable with polishing discs

Splashguard

Shaft and pulleys

Water trough

Coolant overhead feed, or in trough below wheels
Rear mounted motor

Figure 39. A simple mud saw – a method of cutting rocks without using a diamond blade. Steel disc revolves in a tank of mud (thickened slurry of water and silicon carbide loose grits). Speed 400 to 500 rev/min.

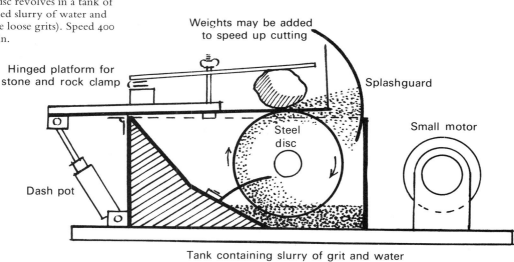

Weights may be added to speed up cutting

Hinged platform for stone and rock clamp

Splashguard

Small motor

Steel disc

Dash pot

Tank containing slurry of grit and water

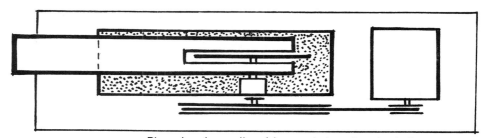

Plan showing pulley drive, and slotted rock platform

The school workshop

In schools and colleges lapidary can be an important subject in its own right or combined with jewellery-making in a shared workshop and a situation such as this may have a generous allowance of working space and material resources for skilful planning. Alternatively, in craft rooms offering several practical activities, lapidary may be limited to a small corner and restricted in scope.

Lapidary work need not be exclusive to art and technical craft departments and can have valuable associations with many other school subjects. Items of equipment such as diamond saws and lapping units are quite often standard aids in preparation of material for scientific or geological research projects. Many such departments prefer small portable lapidary units which can be easily stored when not in use.

In addition to the general considerations outlined previously, planning lapidary craft areas in schools will be subject to stricter controls. Educational authorities may impose slightly differing standards for machine construction and siting but all will be concerned with maximum safety. Many will insist on a copy of accepted workshop safety regulations being displayed in rooms using powered machines. Although most of the lapidary machines manufactured for general purposes are portable, some school authorities require machines to be bolted to a bench or securely clamped in fixed positions during use. In addition, the provision of on/off push buttons or starter switches situated on or close to the machines are often required, with power supplies controlled by a master switch.

Whenever possible benches supporting machines should be against a wall to avoid distraction and movement in front of the operator. Good lighting should be placed above the machines so that shadows are not cast on the work. The siting of machines should be planned to allow a progressive working sequence through sawing, grinding, sanding and polishing with minimum congestion. Processes requiring the use of loose abrasive grits, for example laps for sanding flat sections, should be isolated from polishing areas. Dopping facilities are best situated away from the machines to allow unrestricted working space. A convenient supply of water for coolant and rinsing purposes is essential.

The amount of machinery required will depend to some extent on the number of students but ideally, and in the interests of safety, not more than twelve students should be under the supervision of one tutor.

During the initial cutting period the grinding wheels are in greater demand but the situation eventually eases as students progress through the different stages. For a class of twelve students it should be sufficient to have three grinding machines with attachments for sanding and polishing or incorporating drum or belt sanders. In addition a machine with a horizontal metal lap using loose grits for lapping flat surfaces and which has an interchangeable felt disc for polishing is an advantage, since more than one person may work on it at the same time. If a further machine of this type is available it can be kept solely for polishing and thus save time and inconvenience in changing laps. It is useful to have a diamond saw as a separate unit, preferably with an eight or ten-inch blade so that it can be used for slabbing and trimming. The more specialized crafts of carving and facetting stones require a greater degree of concentration and equipment for these activities should be sited away from the grinding and polishing units.

The lapidary club workshop

Many lapidary clubs are only able to offer their members opportunities for practical work by arrangement with a local school or college where equipment is available. Naturally this limits the scope of activities and in some cases the machines may be inaccessible during school vacations. It is the cherished objective of most lapidary societies to have an independent club workshop where a wide range of lapidary skills and jewellery-making can be practised. In addition, space could be devoted to permanent displays of minerals and fossils, a fluorescent cabinet, a small library of books and magazines, and facilities for refreshments.

Equipment and layout will depend on the area of the workshop and the number of active club members with varied practical skills who are prepared to pool their resources. Quite often a limited budget will call for improvization and with some ingenuity machines for every lapidary process can be constructed by members (figure 40). To meet initial outlay and running costs a charge can be made to those using the equipment and in the case of diamond saws a small fee per inch of material cut will eventually cover the cost of renewing the diamond blade.

As in all workshop situations, strict adherence to safety regulations is essential and clubs should display their own code of workshop practice and conduct. A number of workshop supervisors should be available on an agreed rota system to give assistance to beginners and ensure correct usage of machines. Responsibility for care and maintenance of the workshop is usually undertaken by a sub-committee nominated for the purpose. Another important aspect that should be considered is the insurance of premises and equipment, and liability for claims by members should the occasion arise.

Figure 40. Group workshop. Lapping units in separate bays to prevent contamination of grits

6 Practical
Gem Cutting

This chapter is mainly concerned with various means of producing polished stones which may either be incorporated in jewellery or used as display pieces. None of the processes described requires an inordinate amount of skill and most people manage to achieve satisfactory results at their first attempt. The following pages of instructions are intended to give beginners an insight into the basic techniques of lapidary but no amount of theory can substitute for the valuable lessons learned in practising the craft.

Sawing

With vertical diamond saws the visible area of the blade projecting above the saw bed will determine the scale of rocks to be cut and increased blade diameter will permit slabbing of larger rocks. As a general guide, the upper portion of the rim should remain clear of the rock as cutting proceeds and not be entirely engulfed, thus preventing any over-riding by the uncut portion of the rock. This places undue stress on diamond points and may result in a dished blade. Also, in this situation several cuts will be necessary to complete the slice and a smooth slab, free from saw rings, is rarely possible.

Horizontal saws permit an area of movement during cutting between the blade periphery and the securing collars and the rock to be cut must not exceed this diameter. In many cases, however, the clamping capacity of the rock vice will be a controlling factor.

SLABBING

This operation is carried out on saws with blade diameters from ten inches upwards and reduces larger rocks into a number of parallel slices of uniform thickness which can be trimmed further if desired. In some cases, rock sections are cut for display or detailed examination of the structure.

To ensure maximum rigidity and control of the rock during slabbing a clamp or vice is necessary. This usually forms part of a carriage unit directed forward along a built-in guide rail. The rate of cutting or feed should preferably be controlled by weighted tension or other automatic device. The rock vice on a horizontal saw is supported on a freely moving arm and the clamped rock fed to the blade by manual pressure (figure 41).

Sawing must *never* be done dry and methods of supplying coolant and lubricant to blades depend on machine construction. Vertical blades usually run through coolant contained in a shallow tank below the blade or receive fluids piped to the revolving disc through a motorized circulating system. Where coolant is piped

Figure 41. Rock clamp on horizontal saw

on a revolving blade both sides of the disc should receive equal quantities in order to prevent uneven wear and heat stress.

Coolant fluids for cutting hard, non–absorbent stones should be light oils with low viscosity or an evenly proportioned mixture of light mineral oil and paraffin (kerosene). When slabbing soft or porous materials the use of plain water is preferable since oils may produce problems. Oil absorbed into porous stones is difficult to remove and can affect the quality of polish on finished stones. Darkening or discolouration of the stone may also result from oil absorption and washing in detergent and water or placing stones in a box of degreasing granules immediately after sawing is recommended. For general sawing purposes the lubricant and coolant qualities of mineral oils provide a superior cutting action and prolong the effective life of diamond blades. The coolant level in the tank should cover the tip of the vertical blade about a quarter to one third of an inch.

Shaft speeds for slabbing saws up to 10 or 12 inches in diameter can match motor speeds using corresponding pulley sizes. However, peripheral speeds will increase with larger diameter blades and pulley adjustments may have to be made to provide suitable cutting speeds in accordance with manufacturers recommendations for the scale and type of saw blade.

The automatic feed on vertical saws should be adjusted to compensate for hard or soft rock varieties. This will involve periods of experiment to establish the required cutting pressure

Figure 42. Slab saw. Vice carriage stop and weighted tension details

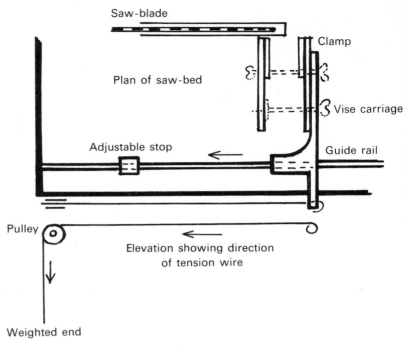

Saw-blade

Plan of saw-bed

Clamp

Vise carriage

Adjustable stop

Guide rail

Pulley

Elevation showing direction
of tension wire

Weighted end

against the blade and the degree of tension on a weighted feed necessary to ensure effective bite of the diamond points.

Rocks should be securely clamped in the vice and tested for any movement. Where the clamp has no base plate the rock must be fixed clear of the saw bed to prevent dragging.

Before switching on the saw, ensure that the coolant level in the enclosed tank is adequate. By turning the blade by hand the amount of oil will be indicated on the rim of the blade. Other cooling systems should be checked. Test the mobility of the rock vice carriage, which must run smoothly along the guide rail. If sticking occurs, the guide rail should be lubricated with light machine oil. Set the vice carriage stop in a suitable position on the guide rail to arrest movement at the end of the cut (figure 42). Ensure the splash-guard over the blade is elevated to clear the top of the clamped rock.

When using weighted feed, switch on the machine but do not immediately engage the tension weights as this will cause the rock carriage to shoot forward and jab the stone against the blade, causing damage to the diamond rim. Take the tension weight in one hand and with the other gently ease the carriage towards the blade and allow cutting to commence, gradually permitting the weight to take over at the correct rate. If the machine has a plastic canopy this should now be fitted in position to contain the fine

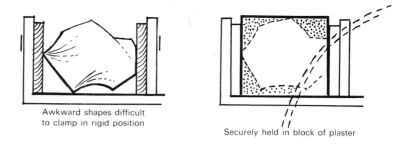

Awkward shapes difficult
to clamp in rigid position

Securely held in block of plaster

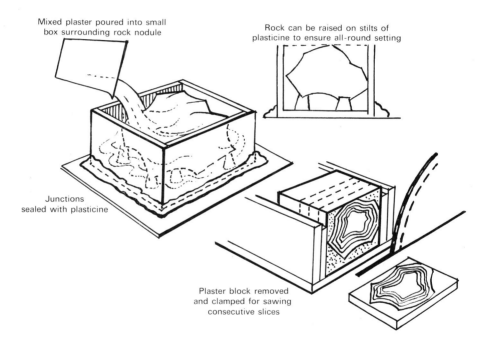

Mixed plaster poured into small
box surrounding rock nodule

Rock can be raised on stilts of
plasticine to ensure all-round setting

Junctions
sealed with plasticine

Plaster block removed
and clamped for sawing
consecutive slices

Figure 43. Embedding awkward shaped pieces of rock in plaster of paris to facilitate clamping in vice

coolant spray. At the end of the cut, draw back the rock carriage clear of the blade, at the same time taking up the tension weight, and switch off the motor.

Most rock clamps have an adjustable slide or cross-feed to position the rock for a number of consecutive slices of even thickness. When a point is reached where the remaining rock or end of a nodule is too small or the wrong shape to be clamped, the rock can be embedded in a block of plaster of paris to aid continued cutting in the clamp (figure 43).

Trim-saws have many uses, from cutting slabs into workable pieces, slicing pebbles and smaller lumps of gemstone rough, or trimming away unwanted portions of cabochon blanks to save grinding. Average trim-saw blades are six to eight inches in diameter with smaller versions for more delicate slitting tasks.

Vertical and horizontal trim-saws function in the same way as the slabbing saws already described but in the case of vertical saws, with coolant tank and flat saw bed, trimming is usually done by hand (figure 44). A rock clamp is still necessary for trimming on horizontal and angled blades.

Oil coolant and lubricant is used as before for general cutting, with plain water as a substitute when cutting soft absorbent materials. For trimming, a water soluble oil is sometimes preferred, but this is less efficient as a cutting aid and may lead to rusting if the machine and blade are not carefully dried after use.

The stone is fed carefully to the revolving blade and eased forward with steady pressure, but not forced, until the cut is

Figure 44. Using a trim saw

completed. With a vertical blade hold the stone flat on the saw bed to prevent the stone rising up the blade and avoid twisting or attempting to cut in a curve. The blades are thin and easily dished with improper use. In a similar way, when cutting into a curved surface such as a pebble, allow the saw to gently nibble a starting point before applying pressure. This will prevent the blade slipping round the curve of the stone. A flat base to the stone will ride more evenly along the saw bed and a ground or previously sawn flat surface will assist the forward movement. Embedding a small pebble in a block of plaster of paris as previously described will serve the same purpose.

When the end of the cut is reached, do not let go of the stone but draw back both halves simultaneously until clear of the blade. If a stone is released at the rear of the blade there is a danger of both pieces being flung forward by the revolving disc.

Although trim-saws can be used for slicing small lumps of rock and pebbles, these should be limited in size to $1\frac{1}{2}$ to 2 inches at the largest dimension for six–inch saws and proportionately less for smaller blades. Ideally, trim–saws should be used exclusively for sectioning and trimming flat slabs up to quarter of an inch thickness, and this will greatly extend the life of the blade.

Polishing flat sections

Thin slabs and sectioned rock nodules required for display are sanded and polished by a horizontal lapping process. The base of cabochons and flat faces of stones cut for jewellery may be similarly treated. For quick results a clean saw cut will save a considerable amount of laborious sanding in the preliminary stages; concentric ridges formed by a saw cutting out of true are difficult to remove.

HAND LAPPING

Methods not involving the use of machinery are often tedious but nevertheless effective for producing flat, polished faces. Equipment is simple and consists of various supports for abrasive grits and polishes.

Materials: Small plate glass slab
Piece of rigid acrylic sheet (Perspex, Lucite)
Silicon carbide loose abrasive grits, coarse to fine
Water, used as coolant/lubricant
A leather pad glued to a board
Small mixing dish
Cerium oxide polishing agent

Stage one. Apply water to the glass plate and sprinkle about a half teaspoonful of coarse 80 or 120 grit over the surface. The amount of moisture should be controlled to prevent grit particles washing off the glass. Hold the stone slab firmly and rotate in circular and figure of eight movements over the entire sanding surface, using moderate pressure. Make sure the stone is held flat and avoid any rocking action which may lead to facets developing on the leading or trailing edge of the stone. Rinse frequently and check progress. The abrasive grits may have to be renewed periodically as the grains break down under pressure. Continue until the surface of the stone is perfectly flat and free from saw marks or other imperfections.

Stage two. Sponge down the glass plate to remove grits and slurry. Wash the stone and hands thoroughly. Apply a finer grade of abrasive (220–320) and repeat the sanding actions as before. Gradually remove all traces of the previous coarse abrasion and continue until the surface texture acquires a uniform appearance.

Again, wash the stone, hands and working surfaces to prevent grit contamination.

Stage three. For surface refinement and pre-polish, a piece of rigid acrylic sheet is used instead of the plate glass. The plastic sheet provides a firm but softer surface, allowing impregnation by the abrasive grains. For this reason it must be kept exclusively for the final sanding phase and protected from the coarser grit particles by storing in a plastic bag.

Dampen the surface and apply 400 or 600 abrasive powder. Sand as before, using additional water and grit when required, until a smooth satin finish is achieved. Wash stone and hands to remove all traces of grit.

Stage four. For the final polishing a piece of thin leather glued rough side uppermost to a firm support is used. Mix a thin slurry of water and cerium oxide powder in a shallow dish and apply to the pad with a soft brush. Do not saturate the polishing pad as this will retard the friction needed to produce a glaze on the surface of the stone.

Rub the stone vigorously on the pad, only replenishing the polish when the surface is drying out. Rinse frequently in clean water and inspect the stone under a good light. Continue the process until a satisfactory polish has been imparted over the entire face of the stone. Rinse well in warm water and liquid detergent.

ALTERNATIVE METHOD OF HAND LAPPING

The same sanding procedure can be carried out using sheets of wet/dry coated abrasive papers or cloths instead of loose grits. Two or three grades will be necessary prior to polishing. It is an advantage to use the silicon carbide coated papers in conjunction

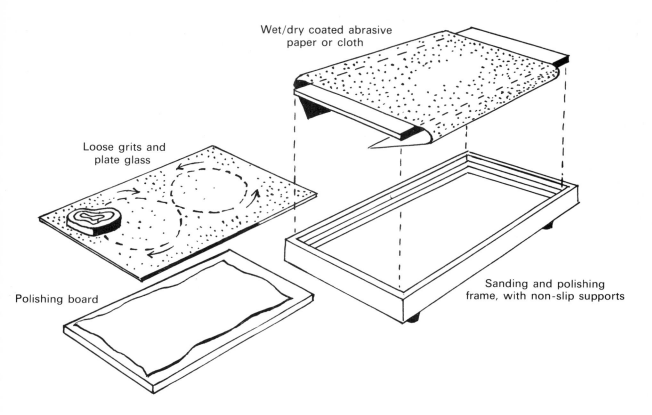

Wet/dry coated abrasive
paper or cloth

Loose grits and
plate glass

Polishing board

Sanding and polishing
frame, with non-slip supports

Figure 45. Frame used to aid sanding and polishing by hand

with a simply constructed sanding frame (figure 45). This helps to prevent wrinkling or tearing the papers during the sanding action. The leather pad used in the polishing stage can be cut to the correct size to fit into the frame.

CAST IRON ROTARY LAP

The lapping procedures are similar to those described for hand lapping but the cutting efficiency of the grits is increased by the revolving lap and two-handed control of the rock slab promotes an even distribution of pressure (figure 46).

Two or three grit stages can be employed as before, for example a triple sequence of 120, 220, 400 grits, or 220, 320, 500 grits, depending on the hardness and surface condition of the stone. In exceptional circumstances it may be necessary to commence with a coarse abrasive such as 80 grit.

The abrasive slurry (grit and water) can be contained in a small dish and applied to the revolving lap with a soft-hair brush. The water serves as coolant/lubricant and a vehicle for the grits. As the particles settle quickly in the container, the slurry should be stirred well to ensure that sufficient grit is transferred to the lap. To charge

Figure 46. Applying grit to cast iron lap

the revolving lap, brush the slurry across the surface from centre to outer rim. During cutting, the lap should be recharged when the 'bite' of the grit is no longer discernible.

When sanding a large slab, hold the stone between thumb and second finger of both hands and apply additional pressure with the first fingers. In this way rocking can be avoided and the leading and trailing edges of the slab will receive equal treatment. Since the speed of the lap increases towards the periphery, the rate of cutting will vary from the centre to the edge of the disc. Allowances must be made for this by moving the stone slab across the lap and reversing the leading and trailing positions. Laps without a central locking nut permit greater freedom of movement. Frequent rinsing and progress checks must be carried out.

At the end of each sanding phase it is necessary only to sponge off the grit and slurry from the lapping plate before proceeding immediately with the finer abrasive.

Following the ultimate sanding stage, wash stone, hands and lap and clean the machine thoroughly to remove traces of grit

Plate 2. Worked examples of
nephrite jade, agate, onyx marble, opal,
bloodstone, amber and turquoise

(Crown copyright. Reproduced by
permission of the Institute of Geological
Sciences)

particles. Replace the metal lap with a felt or leather disc in readiness for final polishing.

A pre-polishing state can also be achieved by carrying out the stages on discs of copper or other soft metals impregnated with diamond. Separate discs with graded micron particles from coarse to fine are used employing the same lapping techniques. Water coolant with a little detergent is applied to the disc as required. With lapping discs of soft metals there is always a danger of sharp edges on the rock slab gouging into the lap surface and ripping out the diamond particles. To prevent this occurring, grind a small bevel round the edges of the slab to enable the stone to ride over the lap surface.

Polishing. Laps for this final treatment should be firm and level and should only be used for the purpose of flat lapping. Polishing cabochons on the same disc will hollow out the lap surface and render it useless for flat contact. Discs of hard felt or leather glued to a rigid backing are suitable materials, allowing moisture absorption and retention of polishing oxides. Saturation of absorbent discs must be avoided as a certain amount of frictional drag is

Figure 47. Polishing on felt lap

needed to impart a glaze to the face of the stone. Excessive moisture leads to negative sliding over the pad.

The polishing medium, cerium oxide or tin oxide as a watery slurry can be applied by brush or from a plastic bottle when renewal of the mixture is indicated. Over-dryness of the polishing disc and increased frictional pull on the stone may lead to surface flaws and internal fractures in heat-sensitive stones.

During polishing, the rock slab is held firmly in both hands with an even distribution of pressure as previously described for sanding (figure 47). Rinse the stone frequently and inspect the surface for any traces of scratches or patches of dullness. If scratches persist it will be necessary to return to one of the earlier abrasive stages. Continue until the stone is polished to satisfaction.

VIBRATING LAPS

With vibratory laps it is possible to process several flat slabs at the same time and once the machine is switched on the sanding action is automatic and apart from progress checks can be left unattended during each abrasive run. The slabs are sanded in a circular oscillating pan which provides sufficient agitation to move the slabs across a flat metal bed charged with abrasives and water. In some cases, channelled grids are cast in the metal plates to permit effective distribution of the abrasive grits. Rubber bumper guards fitted around the perimeter of the pans prevents slabs chipping and assists gradual circulation. A polishing pad of toughened fabric or nylon replaces the lapping plates in the final stages.

Machines must always be operated according to maker's instructions and particular attention must be paid to critical adjustments necessary for accurate balance and levelling of the lapping pans to prevent concentration of the cutting in one area. Abrasion not only cuts into the rock slabs but also wears away the surface of the lap plate, therefore avoidance of uneven wear is vital. Some machines are designed for reversal of worn lap plates.

When sanding a number of slabs at the same time, try to select stones in the same hardness range and of comparable thickness. The surface area of the lapping plate can be covered between 60 and 70 per cent, allowing space for unhindered circulation of the slabs. Blockages can occur if the slabs are angular or sharply pointed, resulting in a tightly wedged mass at the side of the pan, and slabs with a circular or curved perimeter will permit free movement. If slabs remain stationary during the vibratory action there is a danger of the grid pattern from the lap plate becoming engraved on the face of the stones through continued abrasion. Also, in this situation, slabs will tend to ride up and over each other, causing chattering and the likelihood of fractured stones.

No definitive time phases or grit combinations can be quoted but the following general observations will be helpful.

To save hours of coarse sanding it is essential that slabs are sawn cleanly without surface marks or saw rings. Sharp edges should be bevelled to prevent chipping or gouging into the lap.

Grit combinations, applied with water lubricant, can be 80 or 120 for the first stage depending on the hardness of the stones, followed by sequences of 400 grit and 600 grit. Experimentation with different grit combinations can be carried out to advantage. Sanding time can be reduced by weighting the slabs but this should not restrict movement or upset the balance of the lapping plate.

During the sanding phases additional water will be required to compensate for thickening of the slurry and drying out which slows down the cutting action. Additional grit may also be required and regular progress checks are essential.

At the end of each stage, remove the lap plate and immediately wash away all grits and slurry. Clean the rubber cushion ring carefully, particularly when it is used for both sanding and polishing laps.

After the final abrasive stage the face of the slabs should be perfectly smooth with an even, matt surface when held to the light and free from any scratches.

When satisfied that the slabs are ready for polishing, attach the cloth or nylon lap and polish with a slurry of aluminium oxide, tin oxide or cerium oxide. The polishing lap builds up a useful concentration of the polish and need not be washed out at the end of each run unless a change of polishing oxide is desired.

Cutting a cabochon

In order to establish essential lapidary skills and acquire an understanding of equipment and materials involved, cutting a cabochon is perhaps the most suitable and satisfying exercise for the beginner. A gemstone cut 'en-cabochon' is characterized by a smooth polished surface, in marked contrast to the angular geometry of a facetted stone. The smooth, simplified cabochon cut presents the best solution for opaque and translucent stones which are not dependent upon maximum light refraction. Shapes or styles can be round, oval or square in plan and vary in profile from a shallow curve to a steeply formed dome, depending on requirements and nature of the stone (figure 48).

MARKING OUT

Having decided upon the size and type of stone for the cabochon,

Figure 48. Some cabochon profile and base shapes

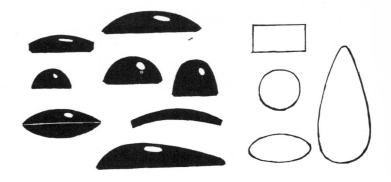

select a suitable piece of rough, slabbed and trimmed to workable proportions, allowing sufficient thickness for the dome. Orientate the stone carefully to utilize the most attractive features in the formation of the dome and prepare to mark out the cabochon base on the reverse side. For this purpose templates are manufactured providing a varied selection of shapes and sizes punched out of a plastic sheet. A thin pointed aluminium pencil can be used to mark out the desired shape (see figures 49–52).

Figure 49. Size of cabochon should be in proportion to thickness of the slab

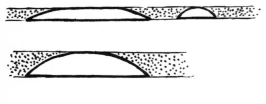

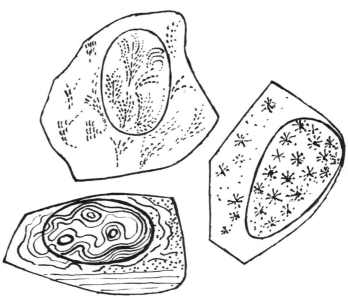

Figure 50. Select most attractive portion of stone for the cabochon dome

Figure 51. Marking out the base shape using a template

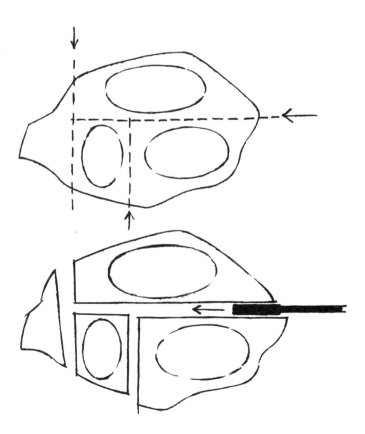

Figure 52. When marking out several shapes on one slab, allow for thickness of the saw blade

Check the driving belt on the lapidary machine to ensure that the correct pulley combination is providing a suitable grinding speed, and switch on the electric motor (figure 53). If the machine is operating two vertical grinding wheels, the 100 or 120 and 220 grit wheels will be adequate for most of the grinding phases. On machines with provision for only one vertical grinding head, the 100 or 120 grit wheel must be used for preliminary grinding. Water coolant should now be introduced, either from a drip feed canister over the wheel or from a trough through which the wheel will revolve.

To grind the base of the cabochon, hold the stone firmly, between finger and thumb of both hands, with the pencilled shape uppermost and in view the whole time. Press the stone against the front, or narrow edge, of the grinding wheel a little below half way, and proceed to grind away unwanted portions of the stone (figure 54). Keep the stone moving across the entire face of the wheel to avoid uneven wear and grooving of the grinding surface. Rinse the stone frequently to clean off any accumulated sludge masking the position of the pencilled base line. Continue grinding as before, turning the stone round in the fingers to ensure even progress, until the base shape has been formed with the pencilled line still visible. At this point, a careful examination of the base should be made to ensure that it is perfectly flat. To clean up the edge of the base, which may be slightly uneven due to flaking in some brittle stones, and to prevent further chipping when sliding the finished stone into a setting, a fine chamfer or

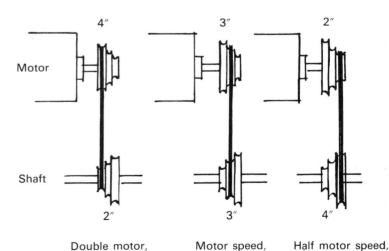

Figure 53. Multiple pulley system for changing machine speeds

Double motor, speed grinding

Motor speed, sanding

Half motor speed, polishing

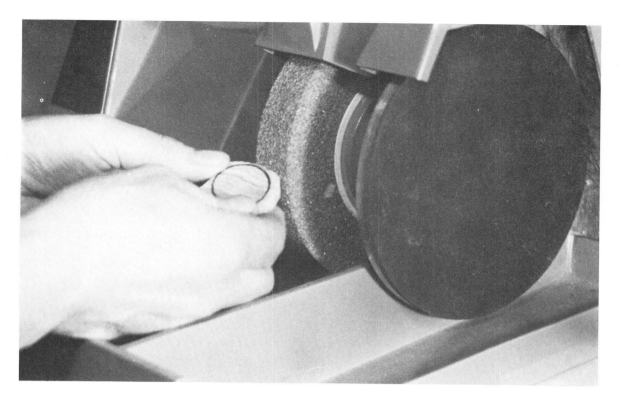

Figure 54. Grinding the base shape

Figure 55. (a) Avoid grooving face of grinding wheel; (b) do not grind into side of wheel; (c) correct use of wheel – grind across entire face

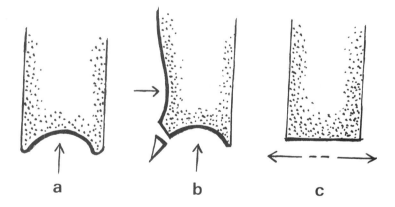

a   b   c

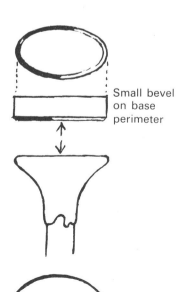

Small bevel on base perimeter

bevel is cut around the perimeter. The stone is now ready for mounting on a dop stick to facilitate grinding and shaping of the cabochon dome (figure 56).

Figure 56. Stone prepared for dopping with fine bevel on base

71

Figure 57. Methods of heating dopping wax: (a) electrically heated dopping oven; (b) gas ring and hot plate; (c) Bunsen burner; (d) spirit lamp and bent metal support; (e) spirit lamp inside inverted can

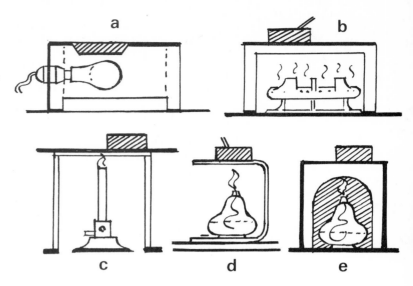

DOPPING THE STONE

Dopping is a method of attaching a stone to a short stick or handle, usually wooden dowelling, using a dopping wax which is basically sealing wax melted with a little powdered shellac. Wax specially manufactured for the purpose can be purchased from lapidary suppliers. The wax gives a strong bond between stone and stick, which enables the lapidary to grind and polish the stone by skilful manipulation of the dop-stick through each process.

To dop the stone, first melt the wax in a shallow tin on a hot-plate heated by a low flame, taking care not to burn. Next, select a suitable piece of dowelling, about six inches in length, and dip the end into the melted wax. Twist the stick to form an even coating of wax and quickly withdraw placing waxed end down on a smooth cool surface. The wax will form a cone at the end of the stick. Place the stone on the hot plate, bevelled side up, and allow to heat gently. Do not over-heat or, in addition to dangers of cracking the stone, messy dopping will result. A small fragment of shellac or dopping-wax placed on the stone will indicate the correct dopping temperature as the wax or shellac starts to run. Take the dop-stick with the now hardened cone of wax and heat the wax until it begins to melt; press the waxed end down on the warmed stone, which should make an instant bond, and lift stone and stick smartly from the hot-plate. Hold the stick upright and centre the stone, moulding the wax to give firm support under the stone (see figures 58, 59, 60). Try to prevent surplus wax forming round the side or on the surface of the stone

Figure 58. Select prepared dopstick to suit size of stone. Warm stone and heat wax on dopstick

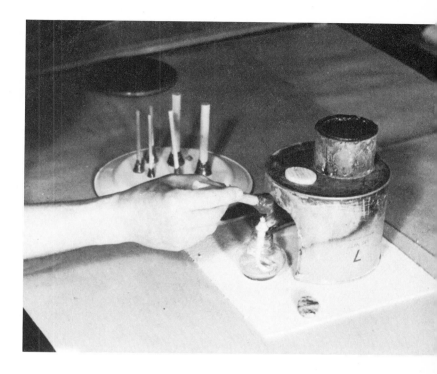

Figure 59. Softened wax pressed on warmed stone

Figure 60. Moulding wax to support stone

Figure 61. Alternative dopping method using dop-wax heater. Wax on dopstick is applied directly to warmed stone.

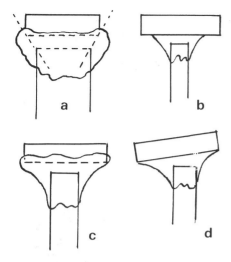

Figure 62. Some common dopping faults: (a) dopstick too thick for stone; (b) dopstick too thin and too little wax; (c) excess wax obscures position of base; (d) off-centre stone – difficult to cut symmetrical cabochon

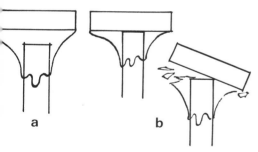

Figure 63. (a) Correctly dopped stone supported on wax; (b) incorrect – if stone rests directly on wood it will be levered off during grinding

as this may influence the final shape of the cabochon (figures 62, 63). Allow sufficient time for the wax to cool naturally before starting to grind the cabochon dome.

Cold Dopping. Stones sensitive to heat can be dopped cold using a paste of dough-like consistency made from cornflour and acetate cement. To prepare a small quantity, place a little of the cement in a dish, add the cornflour and mix into a dough. Model the dough on the end of a dopstick to make a support for the stone, as in the manner of dopping wax, and spread a little cement on the base of the stone to be dopped. Press together and centre correctly, moulding the dough under the stone. Place dopped stone in an upright position and allow to set hard.

Following shaping and polishing the stone can be removed by softening the dough with acetone solvent fluid until the stone will part from the dop without forcing. It should be noted that this method of removal is unsuitable for doublets and triplets which have been cemented together with films of clear acetone adhesive.

SHAPING THE DOME

With the stone securely fixed to a dopstick greater freedom of manipulation is now possible during the subsequent grinding stages. Provisional roughing out and shaping can be done on a 100 or 120 grit grinding wheel, revolving at a suitable speed and supplied with adequate water coolant. Holding the dopstick in both hands, one close to the stone and the other nearer the end of the dopstick, press the stone against the front edge of the grinding wheel at an angle of about forty-five degrees. By turning the dopstick slowly and moving the stone slightly upwards and across the grinding surface, cut a pronounced bevel around the stone, stopping short of the wax. Increase the angle of the dopstick and cut a further bevel, working towards the centre of the stone. By repeating this procedure a rough doming will evolve in a series of angular steps or bands (figures 64 and 65).

The successive grinding should aim at eliminating any suggestion of angles and points on the stone until a smooth, symmetrical dome is formed. This is achieved by continuous rocking and turning the stone against the wheel by manipulating the dopstick, turning with one hand and rotating the end of the stick with the other. Rinse the stone often and check progress under a good light. Continue shaping until the dome is perfectly smooth, paying particular attention to the edge of the stone near the base.

Although relatively smooth and shaped to satisfaction the cabochon dome will show marks and scratches from the 100 or 120 grit wheel at this stage. Surface refinements can be carried out on the finer 220 grit grinding wheel by gently working and turning the stone as before but with greater delicacy of touch and con-

Figure 64. Stages in rounding cabochon dome

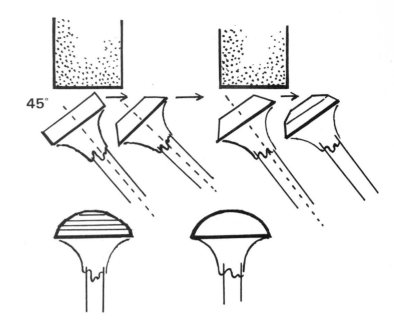

Figure 65. Grinding cabochon dome. Note position of hands

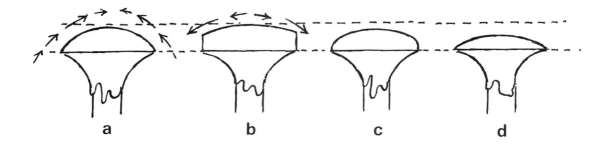

Figure 66. Shaping the dome: (a) correct – always work from base towards top of dome to retain maximum thickness of slab; (b) incorrect – never work from top downwards as this leads to shallow or straight sided cabochons (c, d)

tinuous movement to avoid producing tiny facets. At all times during grinding the stone should be in contact with water coolant. When satisfied that the cabochon dome is of pleasing shape and proportions viewed from all sides, the grinding phases are completed and the stone ready for sanding.

SANDING

The term 'sanding' is used to denote transitional stages between grinding and polishing, although there is no clear division. Abrasion continues during sanding and at the same time polishing or glazing of the surface occurs in some stones. Two popular methods of sanding can be employed, either the use of coated abrasives of paper or cloth or the application of loose abrasive grits to horizontal discs of leather, wood or metal.

Sanding with coated discs. Silicon carbide wet/dry discs are attached to firm backing discs by means of a gum solution, preferably of the easy peel-off type. Good results are obtained by using 220 and 400 grit discs successively but some people prefer to introduce others such as 320, 500 or 600 grades.

Attach a 220 disc to either vertical or horizontal lap and arrange pulley and belt combination to turn the disc at motor speed. Holding the dopstick firmly, apply the cabochon dome to the abrasive disc with a rotating, stroking movement. Keep the stone moving continually to prevent the formation of facets and use plenty of water coolant. Continue sanding until all marks left by previous grinding have been removed. Repeat the process on a 400 grit disc, which is normally enough to complete the sanding operation. The stone should now be perfectly smooth and in some cases will have acquired a slight polish (figure 67).

Belt and drum sanders. When using machines with drum sanders the action and handling of the dopstick is similar to that used for grinding and follows a natural progression through the abrasive stages. The dopstick can be manipulated with both hands and a rocking, sweeping motion of the stone against the sanding

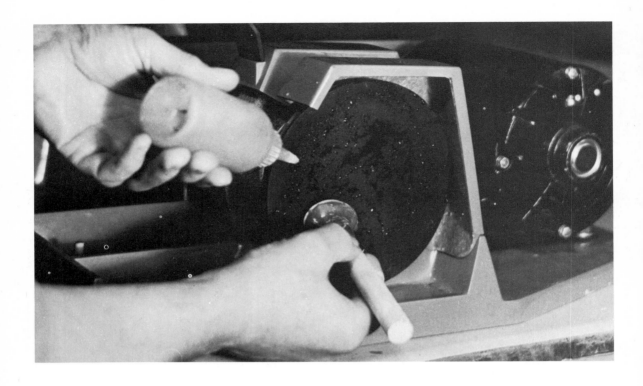

Figure 67. Sanding cabochon on wet/dry abrasive discs. Water coolant applied from plastic bottle as required

surface will prevent formation of facets. Water coolant is usually piped to the drums from overhead control valves.

Depending on the machine type, sanding sleeves of coated paper or cloth can be continuous bands which slip over the padded drum, usually rubberized, or strips which wrap round the drum and clip tightly into a junction on the rim. A range of abrasive grit sizes is available, as for coated discs, and the drums revolve at the same sanding speeds. The resilience of the padded drum conforms to the cabochon shape and aids the sanding process.

Continuous belt sanders operate on separate machines, making different sanding positions possible by adjusting the angle of the sanding face.

Sanding with loose grits. Considerably slower machine speed is necessary when using grit powder on a horizontal lap. Leather laps running at approximately half motor speed will permit the grit particles to remain on the discs and become embedded in the leather as work proceeds. A mixture of silicon carbide grit powder and water is applied to the revolving disc, either by a brush or from a plastic bottle, and the stone and dopstick manipulated as described in the previous method. Excellent results are obtained by using three grades of grit, 220, 320 and 500, in succession. A separ-

Figure 68. Sanding on horizontal abrasive surface

ate disc is required for each grade of grit and these should be stored away carefully between stages to prevent mixed grit particles (figure 68).

Use of diamond abrasives

Silicon carbide abrasives followed by various polishing oxides are usually satisfactory for general lapidary purposes but powdered diamond and diamond compounds are also used by both professional and amateur cutters for smoothing and polishing cabochons. Some cutters combine the two methods; pre-forming the cabochon on a grinding wheel, sanding on wet/dry discs until perfectly smooth, followed by polishing on laps charged with fine diamond polishing compounds. Although more expensive than the usual polishing agents, a small quantity of diamond will polish a large number of cabochons and may prove more economical over an extended period.

Laps of fine-grained wood such as maple, grooved to fit various cabochon sizes, can be used in the early stages of smoothing. A coating of wax should be worked into the surface of the wood to retain diamond particles. Final polishing stages can be carried out with diamond compounds on such materials as leather, felt or padded muslin stretched over a support and the surface well impregnated with beeswax. In order to provide a resilient surface for the curvature of the cabochon, a rubber pad should be glued to the backing to cushion the lap material. Separate laps must be kept for each grade of diamond used and these should be stored in polythene bags or other dust-proof containers. It is important to mark the diamond mesh number on the back of each lap and on the container. As a general guide, the larger micron sizes 45, 30 and 15 are used for smoothing and the smaller sizes 3 and 1 for polishing (see table of diamond grit and micron sizes on page 24). A special extender is available to thin the diamond compound and assist in spreading it over the lap surface.

There are machine units manufactured for use solely with diamond abrasives (figure 69) which have a series of interchangeable discs of rigid phenolite and these are charged with diamond by pressure from a small roller to embed the particles. Padded discs are used for polishing and these are glued into position so they can be peeled off and replaced with new pads when necessary. Fine micron diamond is smeared on the pad with the fingertips.

Alternatively, sanding and polishing with diamond is carried out on machines with a row of concave rollers mounted on a horizontal shaft, allowing progression from coarse to finer micron grits. Composition of the rolls on machines of this type

Figure 69. 'Diamond-Miser' – a small sanding and polishing unit for use with diamond compounds. Interchangeable discs. Direct motor drive. Ran-co Products, Granada Hills, California

are of wood or toughened masonite. To charge with diamond, place dots of compound all round the roll and move the dopped stone against the surface, turning the roll over by hand until the diamond is evenly distributed and embedded. Care must be taken not to transfer any of the coarser diamond particles to the fine micron rolls.

Final polishing

Following the sanding phases the cabochon should be ready for a final polish. In order to determine this, wash and dry the stone and carry out a careful inspection to make sure the surface is quite smooth and free from imperfections. It should be emphasized that deep scratches cannot be successfully removed during polishing and in some cases it may be necessary to continue with fine sanding or even return to an earlier stage. Before commencing polishing, wash the stone, hands and working surfaces to remove any traces of abrasive, particularly when loose grit powders have been used, and store away sanding discs or laps.

Machine speeds used for polishing are often a matter of personal choice and experience but half the motor speed will give satisfactory results in most cases and facilitate easy handling of the stone. Various polishing surfaces can be used to suit different types of stones but two popular materials for laps are leather and felt. Beginners should be prepared to experiment with several laps to find which are most suited to particular stones. It will also be found that some stones acquire a good polish on fine grade or well-worn sanding discs.

Most stones in the quartz range will take a good polish on felt polishing discs but care must be taken to avoid excessive pressure on the disc in order to minimize the effect of frictional heat. Stones subjected to over-heating in this way can break or fracture badly, which is very disheartening at this stage. Additionally, in transparent and translucent stones a permanent 'bloom' or internal clouding may result from a frictional burn. Heat-sensitive stones such as opal and turquoise, and varieties susceptible to undercutting, will respond much more successfully on leather polishing discs.

A polishing agent such as cerium oxide, tin oxide or aluminium oxide is mixed with a little water to form a thin paste and brushed on the revolving lap. Holding the dopstick with the fingers close to the mounted stone, slowly rotate the cabochon against the lap surface with light to moderate pressure. With practice a suitable polishing technique will evolve and this may fluctuate between a rocking, rotating movement and a stroking action, working against the direction of the lap. Add more polish

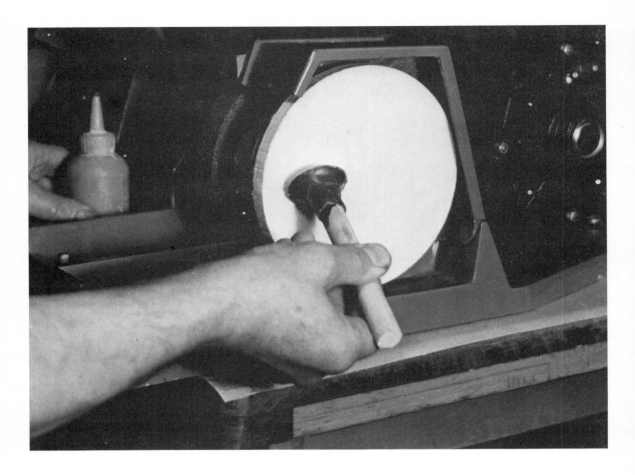

Figure 70. Polishing on felt disc with either tin oxide or cerium oxide

Figure 71. Some faults to avoid when shaping cabochon dome: (a) correct shape; (b) sides too steep for wrap-over bezel setting; (c) flat top to dome; (d) unpolished wavy edge, due to excessive wax; (e) asymmetrical shape, due to off-centre dopping; (f) too shallow, with sharp edges which will chip easily

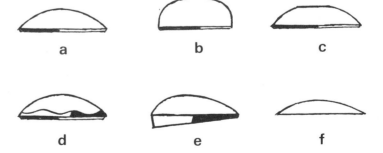

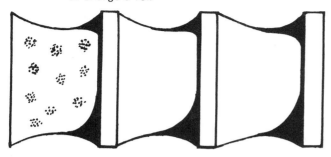

Apply small dots of diamond compound around the roll. About one-half gram of compound required to charge a roll

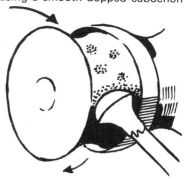

Turn the rolls by hand and spread the diamond particles using a smooth dopped cabochon

Figure 72. Charging sanding and polishing rolls with diamond

as required but do not over-soak; should the lap become saturated the stone will merely slide over the surface and retard the polishing process. Continue until a satisfactory even polish has been imparted to the entire cabochon dome. Particular attention should be paid to the rim of the cabochon by holding the dopstick almost parallel to the lap surface and slowly turning the stone against the disc (figure 70).

To remove the stone from the dopstick, warm the wax over a low flame without over-heating the stone. Using a cloth to protect the fingers from burning, twist the stone free from the wax. Any remaining wax can be carefully scraped off or dissolved with methylated spirits. Alternatively, place the dopstick in a refrigerator for a few minutes to loosen the bond between stone and dopping wax.

If a polished cabochon base is required it can be done by holding the stone against the sanding and polishing discs in turn, taking care not to damage the polished dome.

Facetting

A stone held in a fixed position against a revolving lap will develop a flat surface at the point of contact. The length of cutting time and degree of pressure applied to the stone will determine the area and depth of cut, and the geometric shape of the facet will depend on the angle between stone and lap and perimeter shape of the pre-form. By using facetting aids ranging from simple hand devices to sophisticated machines it is possible to place facets in any desired position around a piece of gem mineral and, equally important, to repeat precisely the order and angles of

Figure 73. A wide selection of gemstone
shapes cut and polished for jewellery

Figure 74. Modifications of Brilliant cut

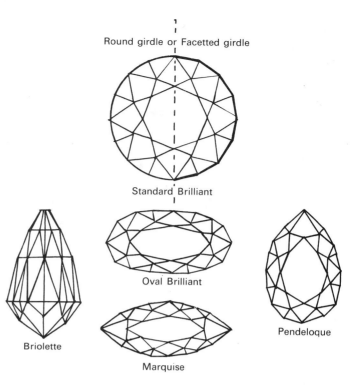

Round girdle or Facetted girdle

Standard Brilliant

Oval Brilliant

Briolette

Marquise

Pendeloque

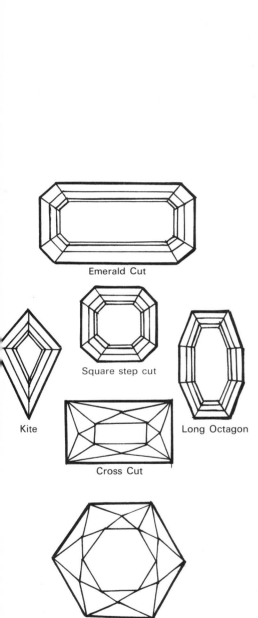

Emerald Cut

Square step cut

Kite

Cross Cut

Long Octagon

Hexagonal Star

Figure 75. Step and geometric cuts

subsequent abrasive and polishing stages. The ordered distribution of facets results in distinctive shapes or styles, many of which are modifications of basic gem cuts. (Figures 74, 75) Stones cut in this way have an upper portion (crown) usually with a larger flat or table facet to permit entry of light, and a lower section (pavilion) cut in such a way as to form an internal barrier deflecting the course of light rays (figure 76). The reflected light re-emerges through the crown facets with scintillating brilliance or 'fire' as the stone is moved. Polished faces of the crown facets also provide highly reflective surfaces.

A style of cut is selected to enhance the colour and refractive properties of the mineral, which in turn determines the proportions of the stone. Natural brilliance can be diminished by misplaced and badly cut facets allowing leakages and dissipation of light values within the stone. Inadequate polishing of facet surfaces, resulting in diffusion of light, will also detract from a stone's colour and brilliancy. Many deeply coloured stones are cut to shallower proportions, deviating from standard measurements for the type of material, to allow greater illumination within the stone. The appearance of weakly coloured stones can be improved slightly by allowing greater depth and increased angles in the pavilion facets.

As an introduction to facetting, a piece of crystalline quartz

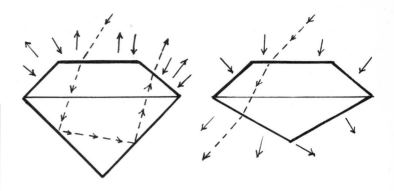

Figure 76. (Left) Refraction of incident light ray giving internal reflection. Light enters and leaves stone through crown facet surfaces. (Right) Loss of incident light ray when stone is cut at incorrect angles

such as clear rock crystal, uniformly coloured amethyst, citrine or pale smoky quartz can be used, and problems of orientation are not involved since quartz has no pronounced cleavage. Any ruined practice stones will be no great loss as quartz facetting material is relatively cheap and easily obtained. To gain basic skills and relate functional aspects of the machine parts to facetting processes, three or four attempts at a standard brilliant cut from quartz are often recommended before progressing to more exotic gem materials or other styles of cut.

Machine Speeds. Lap speeds should not be high and will vary with type of gem material being cut; about 300 rev/min. for cutting and in some cases as low as 100 rev/min for polishing. As a rule slower speeds should be used for soft stones and those of easy cleavage, while faster speeds may be used for harder stones. Experience will indicate the cutting rate desirable for control and prevention of over-cutting the facets. Many machines are constructed to allow speed changes and a further variation can be made by cutting on the outer or inner area of the lap.

TYPES OF LAP

Gem-cutters have their own preferences regarding types of laps and abrasives and the following are some of the most popular. Copper, steel, lead and cast iron laps used with loose silicon carbide grits, 400 to 600 grades, are effective for cutting many types of stones. For the beginner, cast irons laps and silicon carbide abrasive will provide a cheap and suitable method of cutting quartz. With this method scrupulous attention to cleanliness is essential to prevent grit contamination. The disc and master lap must be washed between grit phases and machine parts susceptible to rusting should be dried and wiped with an oily cloth. It is possible to use just one abrasive grade for quartz, such as 400 or 500 grit, which obviates the need to clean the machine repeatedly as would be necessary if two grit stages were used.

Using copper laps impregnated with diamond particles eliminates the cleaning problems associated with loose grits. Two copper laps with 400 or 600 grade diamond grits embedded in the metal surface can be used with water coolant or refined oils for the first cutting and 1200 grade for refinements prior to polishing. Diamond laps are cleaner and faster, without risk of grit contamination or rusting and are favoured by many cutters. Diamond compounds in a similar grit range are also used on copper discs and applied as required, together with a special extender. Renewal of diamond grit is usually indicated when a coppery glaze from the lap surface appears on the facets. It is recommended that when using two-stage cutting the facets are only partially cut with the coarse abrasive grit and completed with the finer grade to prevent over-cutting.

Discs for polishing can be cut from various hard materials. Thick acrylic sheet, copper, tin-faced and type-metal laps are used, in some cases scored with a knife to retain polishing oxides. Scoring the lap surface of metal discs is not always advantageous and unless the metal burrs are carefully levelled severe scratching of the facets can result. Beginners to facetting should experiment with both scored and unscored laps. Other laps can be made of hardwood sealed with beeswax, or muslin and closely woven canvas stretched over a firm support and impregnated with wax to give a smooth surface. Polishing laps should be firm, as too much resilience in the surface and too much pressure on the stone may result in a rounding of facet edges (figure 77).

Tin oxide, cerium oxide, chrome oxide and aluminium oxide are polishes used successfully under varying circumstances and applied to laps as a water-based slurry. Cerium oxide is an excel-

Figure 77. Preparation of lap surfaces: (a) to impregnate with diamond compound, apply lightly in a series of dots from applicator and spread over disc with finger. Pressure from a small hard roller or smooth agate slab will embed diamond particles in lap surface; (b) Laps for polishes should be scored with a sharply pointed knife. Raised burrs must be smoothed away

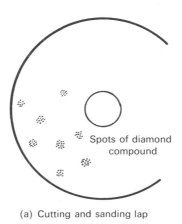

Spots of diamond compound

(a) Cutting and sanding lap

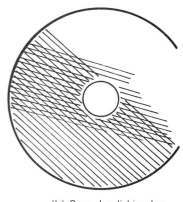

(b) Scored polishing lap

lent general purpose polish and ideal for quartz when used on acrylic laps. Fine micron diamond compound, 8000 to 14 000, mesh is used as an alternative polishing medium particularly with harder gemstones. Diamond compounds are spread from syringe-type applicators over the surface of the lap as required and a special extender fluid or light mineral oil is used as a lubricant.

THE FACETTING MACHINE

A facetting unit usually consists of an accurately balanced *master lap* set on a *vertical shaft* driven by a $\frac{1}{4}$ or 1/6 hp motor. A shallow *splash pan* surrounds the lap and, in some cases, the height is adjustable to allow clearance for the dop arm at certain angles. The support for the master lap and shaft is attached to a substantial *base* which also holds the *mast* for the *facetting arm,* giving equal rigidity and vertical alignment of mast and shaft. The mast, or stand rod as it is sometimes termed, can be moved forwards or backwards on the base and secured in position by a locking nut.

Masts can be tubular or notched and grooved but must be accurately machined to fit the sleeve of the facetting head so that it may be raised and lowered in relation to the lap and cutting angle. A trigger catch or locking nut secures the facetting head in the required position on the mast.

The facetting head has a *pivotting arm* with an *index gear* at one end which can be engaged with a trigger catch when cutting numbered facets. The lower end of the arm has a *chuck* to secure the *dopstick* and stone. The index gear has numbered teeth which are used to space the facets accurately around the stone in their correct position and order according to the formula worked out for the particular cut. Correct angles for the facets are selected on a *quadrant arc* engraved with 90 degrees (figure 78).

PRE–FORMING

Rough gem material is usually pre-formed to the basic shape of a particular style or cut to remove quickly unwanted portions of the stone. Excess material can first be removed by judicious use of a fine trim-saw, followed by grinding on a 220 grit silicon carbide grinding wheel. In the case of small crystals and material carefully trimmed to remove any sharp points which could gouge into the lap, it is possible to pre-form directly on the facetting lap.

Having selected a suitable piece of crystal consider the desired proportions of the finished stone and decide on the position of the top or table, allowing sufficient width for girdle dimensions. With quartz varieties the table can be placed in any convenient position within the crystal but for other gem materials the particular properties of cleavage must be considered. The pre-form

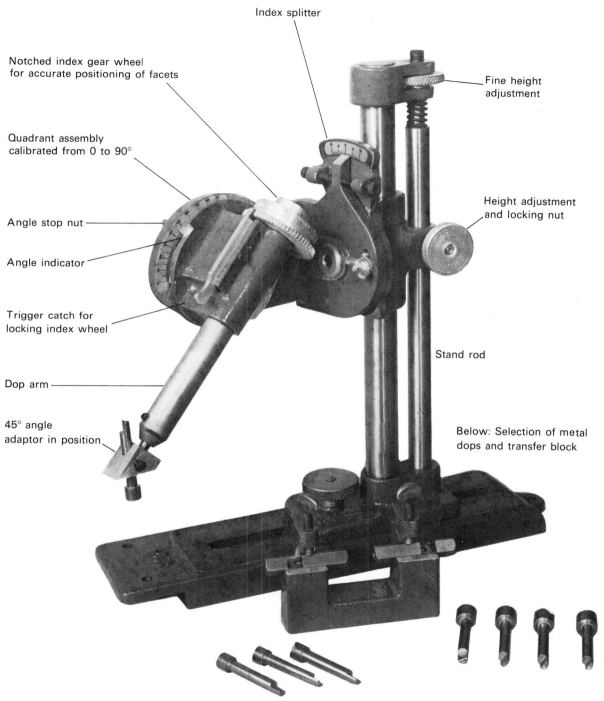

Index splitter

Notched index gear wheel
for accurate positioning of facets

Fine height
adjustment

Quadrant assembly
calibrated from 0 to 90°

Angle stop nut

Angle indicator

Height adjustment
and locking nut

Trigger catch for
locking index wheel

Dop arm

Stand rod

45° angle
adaptor in position

Below: Selection of metal
dops and transfer block

Figure 78. Details of a typical facetting
head

89

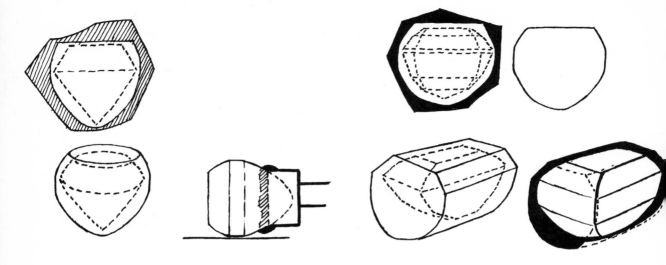

Figure 79. Round Brilliant pre-form.
Girdle cut at 90°

Figure 80. Step cut pre-form

should only approximate the shape of the finished gem and attempts to guess the main angles of the crown and pavilion may lead to cutting away vital material, resulting in a smaller stone. This can be an important factor when using expensive gem rough (figures 79, 80).

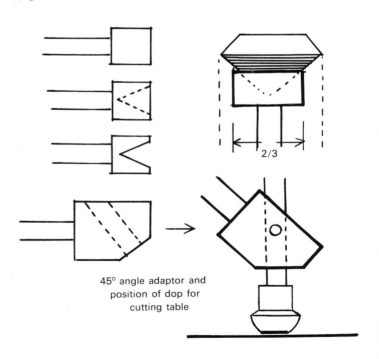

45° angle adaptor and
position of dop for
cutting table

Figure 81. Metal dop shapes

Facetting a stone with crown and pavilion areas involves two distinct dopping stages. With a standard round, brilliant cutting priority for crown or pavilion is a matter for personal choice but whichever order has been decided upon the preform must be held securely in a special dop. Secondly, the stone must be accurately reversed by transfer to another dopstick for cutting the opposite series of facets. The dopsticks are made of metal and shaped at the ends to suit different styles of cut and having a diameter about one third less than the stone's gridle (figure 81).

The means of heating dopping wax are the same as those for general dopping purposes used for cabochons and the wax is a mixture of sealing-wax and shellac. For small gems shellac alone will have sufficient adhesion on a flat table facet to enable pavilion facets to be cut. The pre-form and tin of wax can be heated in the usual way, taking care not to over heat the stone or boil the wax.

Dopping a standard round brilliant for cutting crown facets first. Method:

(1) Select dop and warm end in flame of spirit lamp or butane torch.
(2) Using a small stick, drip a little softened wax into conical end of the dop. Allow for displacement of wax when stone is inserted.
(3) Push the tapered end (pavilion) of the preform, previously heated, into the softened wax until the stone is seated on the metal dop. Centre carefully (figure 82).

The wax displaced can be moulded under the girdle of the stone. Any surplus wax which may have run over the crown area can be removed by a warmed knife blade and wiped clean with spirit solvent.

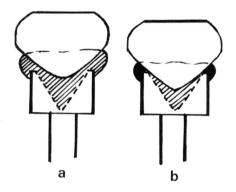

Figure 82. Dopping a Brilliant pre-form: (a) incorrectly seated due to excessive wax; (b) correctly seated in metal dop

TRANSFER DOPPING

When the crown facets are cut the stone is reversed. This is usually accomplished by using a transfer jig consisting of two blocks fixed a short distance apart with horizontal grooves cut in perfect alignment to hold two dopsticks. Locking-plates and screws secure the dops in the grooves.

Alignment of crown and pavilion facets is essential in a correctly cut stone and this is made possible at the transfer dopping stage. It is a simple matter when the metal dops are constructed to fit into special slots and grooves in the facetting arm chuck, preventing any movement in either direction. When cutting is recommenced following transfer, whichever half of the stone is to be cut, the crown and pavilion main facets will correspond automatically at the same index.

Where dops are free to rotate in the chuck, secured perhaps only by a grub screw, the problem is not quite so simple and the position of each main facet will have to be indicated on the girdle of the stone, or marks made on the dop to line up with a similar mark on the facetting arm.

To transfer the stone:

(1) Insert new dop prepared with wax into one groove and secure old dop with stone into opposite groove.

(2) Using spirit lamp or butane torch gently heat the metal and wax of the new dop (figure 83).

(3) Release securing screw and slide old dop forward, pressing crown table into melted wax of new dop. Secure both dops and mould the wax on new dop to give support under girdle of stone. Allow to cool and set (figure 84).

(4) Remove dops from transfer block, bonded together by hardened wax. Warm over a flame, avoiding direct heat on stone. Allow flame to heat the metal end of old dop to soften wax holding the pavilion end of pre-form. (This stage can be carried out with dops still in jig if preferred.)

(5) When the wax melts, gently ease the newly dopped stone away from the old dop. Allow to cool. (Figure 85).

Figure 83. Heating metal and wax of new dop

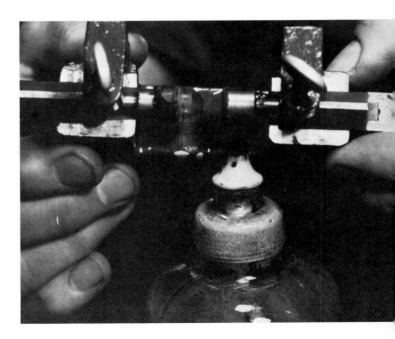

Figure 84. Pressing crown table into melted wax of new dop

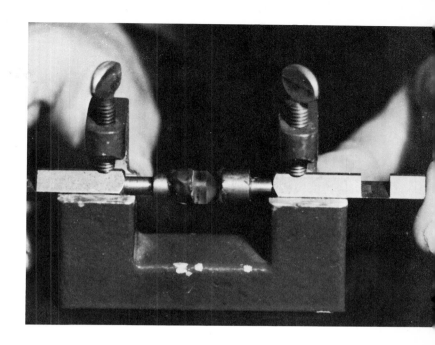

Figure 85. Dops removed from transfer block. Wax of old dop heated to release transferred stone ready for cutting pavilion

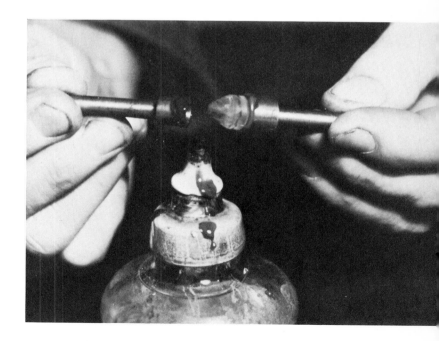

When the wax has hardened, clean off unwanted wax from the stone to ensure that the girdle area is fully exposed to allow unimpeded cutting of the girdle facets.

For stones other than the round brilliant, for example ovals, cushion shapes and pendaloques, it is recommended that the pavilion facets are cut first and the pre-form dopped accordingly. This enables inspection through the table or upper facets when cutting the crown (following transfer), particularly in stones where the pavilion culet is not central.

Standard round brilliant

CUTTING SEQUENCES (see figures 86 and 87)

Select the cutting lap for the chosen method and secure in position on the master lap of the facetting machine. Adjust pulley speeds. Apply grit and water to lap or lubricant to diamond lap as needed. The cutting angles given are for quartz using 64–tooth index gear (figure 88).

ROUNDING THE GIRDLE

Insert dop with mounted stone into chuck of facetting arm and lower unit until the arm is parallel to the lap. The girdle of the stone will now be at 90 degrees. On some machines a section of the lapping pan is detachable for this purpose (figure 89).

Release the index gear catch to allow the facetting arm to turn freely, start the motor and commence trimming the girdle. Turn the arm slowly until every part of the girdle is cut and in contact with the lap (figure 90). Traverse the facetting arm from rim to centre of the lap, applying light pressure to prevent uneven wear or gouging of the lap surface. This cutting action must be used for every subsequent facetting stage. Raise the head assembly and switch off the motor. Replace the lap pan section.

CUTTING THE TABLE

Set the facetting arm at angle of 45 degrees. To position the table parallel to the lap the dopstick is held in a 45 degree angle adaptor which fits into the chuck of the facetting arm (figure 81).

Lower the arm on the stand rod until the stone is in contact with the lap and lock in position. Pivot the arm upwards until clear of the lap then switch on the motor. When the lap is rotating and suitably charged with abrasive, lower the arm and commence cutting the table facet. Traverse the lap surface using lubricant or applications of grit and water as appropriate.

Cut the table to about 70 or 65 per cent of the total width of the preform at this stage, which will be further reduced to 50/45

STANDARD BRILLIANT Crown Facets

Consecutive cutting order, 32 facets

Main Facets, Angle 45° to 42°

Star Facets, Angle 30°/27°

64 tooth gear

Calculate approx 15° less than the Mains

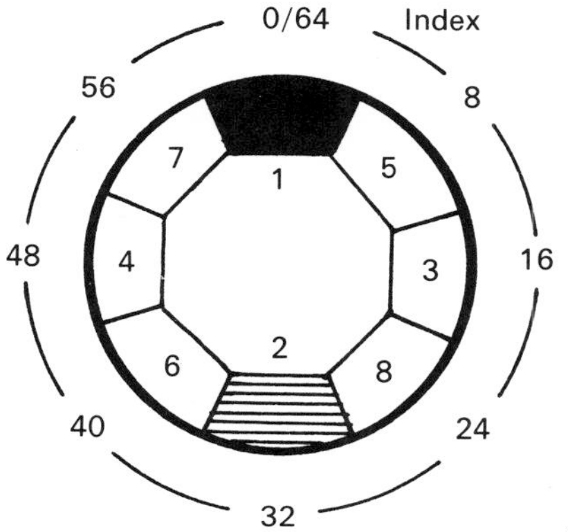

Order	Index
1	64
2	32
3	16
4	48
5	8
6	40
7	56
8	24

Order	Index
9	4
10	12
11	20
12	28
13	36
14	44
15	52
16	60

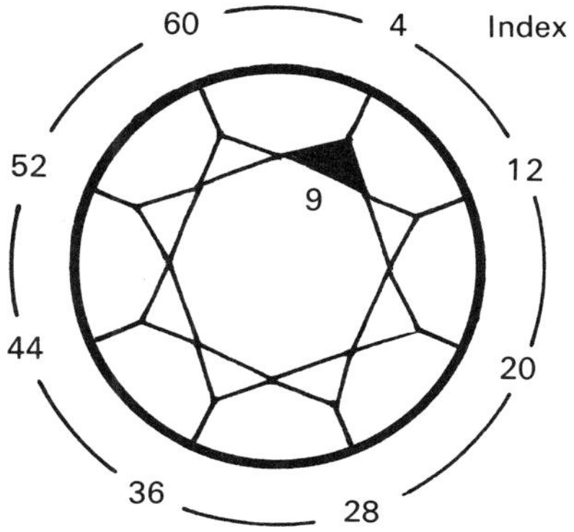

Girdle Facets, or skill facets
Angle 47° plus

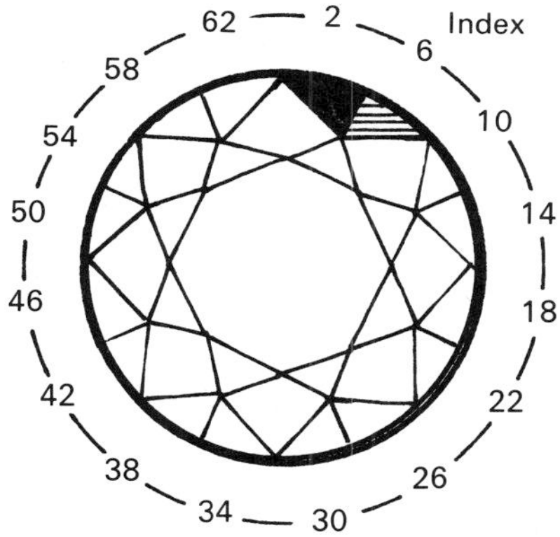

Crown proportions

Order	Index
17	2
18	6
19	10
20	14
21	18
22	22
23	26
24	30

Order	Index
25	34
26	38
27	42
28	46
29	50
30	54
31	58
32	62

50%

1/3

2/3

Angle of girdle facets can
be 2° to 5° more than the
mains angle, or even higher
in a larger stone. Work up in
easy stages

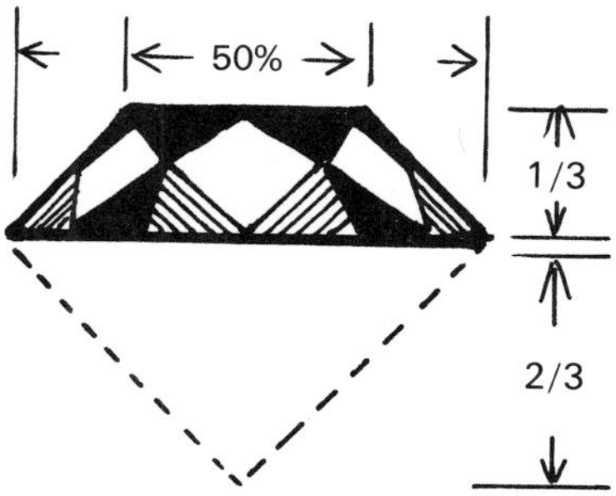

Figure 86. Diagram of cutting sequence
(crown)

STANDARD BRILLIANT   Pavilion Facets

Consecutive Cutting Order, 24 facets

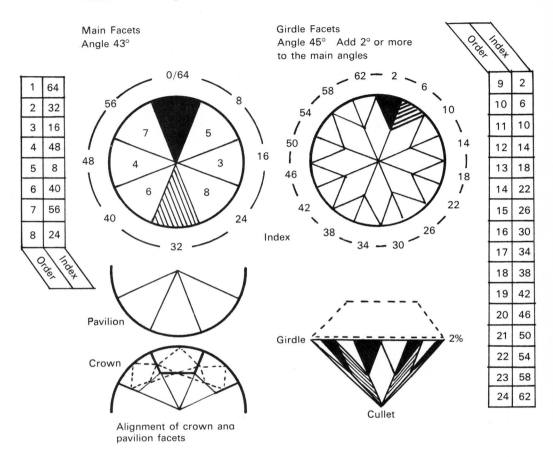

Order	Index
1	64
2	32
3	16
4	48
5	8
6	40
7	56
8	24

Main Facets
Angle 43°

Girdle Facets
Angle 45°   Add 2° or more
to the main angles

Order	Index
9	2
10	6
11	10
12	14
13	18
14	22
15	26
16	30
17	34
18	38
19	42
20	46
21	50
22	54
23	58
24	62

Pavilion

Crown

Alignment of crown and pavilion facets

Girdle   2%

Cullet

Figure 87. Diagram of cutting sequence (pavilion)

per cent in the completed stone. The size of the table can be manipulated for various reasons by increasing or decreasing the angle of the main facets. When the whole of the table surface is uniformly flat and cut to desired dimensions raise the facetting head and switch off the motor. If a two-stage cutting procedure is used, replace the lap with a finer grade and continue cutting to achieve necessary surface refinements for polishing.

If the table facet is polished at this stage it will permit internal inspection of the stone. Remove the cutting disc and clean away all traces of grit on the machine. Place the selected polishing lap in position, switch on the motor and apply a small amount of the appropriate polishing compound. Lower the facetting arm

Figure 88. Conversion chart showing numerical sequences and relative index positions for 96, 64 and 48 index gears

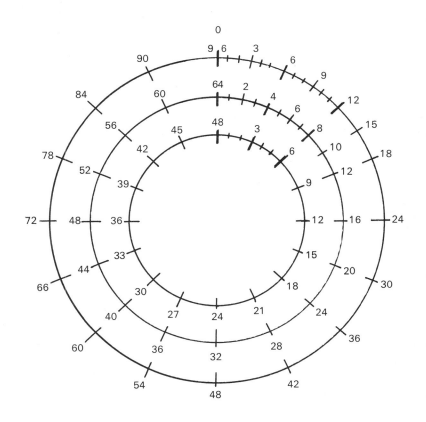

Figure 89. Detachable section of lapping pan

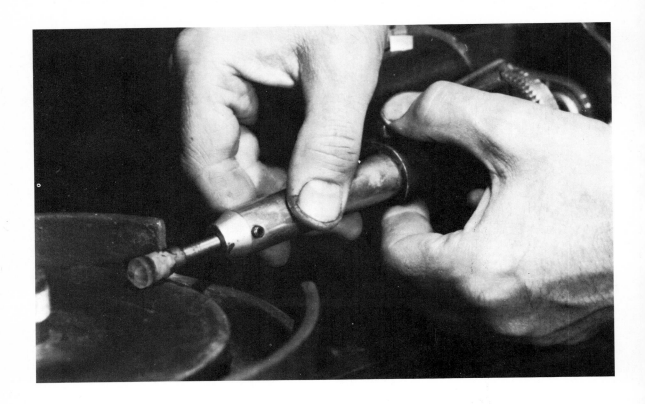

Figure 90. Rounding the girdle. The trigger index catch is held to allow free rotation of facetting arm

and bring the stone into contact with the lap, moving across the lap using moderate pressure to prevent overheating which could soften the wax and dislodge the stone. Frictional heat can be partly controlled by varying the pressure and polishing speed or alternating the position of the stone between the outer and inner portion of the disc. Carry out frequent inspections by pivoting the arm upwards for examination against a good light. A magnifying lens will help to reveal traces of finer scratches which must be removed for perfect results. Polish until a flawless mirror finish is achieved.

Raise the facetting head and switch off the motor. Remove the 45 degree adaptor from the chuck and withdraw the dopstick. Insert the dopstick directly into the facetting arm ready to cut the remaining crown facets. Store the polishing lap away in a plastic bag for protection.

CROWN MAIN FACETS

These are eight in number. Attach the cutting lap, start motor, and apply abrasive slurry or lubricant for selected process. Engage index notch at 0 (64) and set the angle of the facetting arm at

Figure 91. Cutting the main facets

45 degrees. The finished angle may be less than this, allowing for any adjustments which have been necessary to produce adjacent sharp–edged facets. (Figure 91).

Cut the first facet for a short time, then cut the opposite facet indexed at 32, for a similar length of time. Next cut facets three and four indexed at 16 and 48. Cutting opposite facets in this way and alternating between the two for short periods will enable a controlled check to be made on the progressive alignment and proportions of the facets. A stage of cutting will be reached when only the lightest pressure for a fraction of a second will be needed to link the eight facets in sharp ridges from table to girdle.

If angle adjustments have been made during cutting these must be carefully recorded for subsequent cutting and final polishing. It is not necessary to polish until all the remaining crown facets have been cut.

STAR FACETS

In small stones these facets are minute and a single touch to the lap can complete the cut. A second too long or miscalculated pressure will overcut some of the facets and destroy the overall symmetry. Correction may only be possible by re-cutting the main facets and reducing the stone's size.

Index the star facets halfway between the setting for the mains, for example commence at index number 4 on the 64 teeth gear (see diagram figure 88). The facets are inverted triangles with the base edges cutting across the corners of the main facets and touching each other round the table. The inverted points of the triangles are on the ridge lines formed by adjacent main facets, reaching about one-third down. Angles required to position the facets in this way should be recorded for later polishing stages and will be determined as cutting proceeds. Constant checking and frequent adjustments must be made to centre the apex of the triangle on the ridge and control the even spread of the base line to a point where neighbouring facets will touch at the table. If it becomes evident that the broad wedge of the facet will not touch at the centre of the mains before the points reach the one-third limit the cutting angle is probably too high and will have to be dropped one or two degrees. To aid this progress check, commence by cutting two adjacent star facets a little at a time, alternating between the two (index 4 and 12) and work out the angle most suited to requirements. Once the pattern has been established the rest of the facets can be cut in rotation around the girdle.

A suitable starting angle for quartz star facets is 30 degrees, calculated on a subtraction of 15 degrees from the main angle (assuming they were cut successfully at 45 degrees). The dimensions of the stone will influence the finishing angle. As the star facets are so small only one abrasive stage (finer grade) may be required for the purpose. The table area will now have been reduced to its final proportions.

GIRDLE FACETS

There are sixteen triangular girdle facets placed with the base of the triangles forming the girdle, one facet at each side of the eight mains ridges. The apex of the triangles touch the points of the star facets approximately two-thirds of the distance between girdle and table.

Cutting angles can be set for 47 degrees as a 'feeler' but for accurate positioning the correct angle may be a few degrees more or less than this. Index at 2 followed by 6 (64 gear). Proceed to cut pairs of facets gradually, using the lightest touch for half a second, pivot the arm upwards to check progress, and repeat the cutting action. Alternate between the two matching pairs and estimate the rate of triangular spread. Adjust the angle if the height of the apex is cutting too rapidly compared to the base. When the angled base points meet in the centre of the main facet and the apex of the two triangles coincides at the tip of the star facets, the correct angle will have been reached. Carefully record and cut any remaining facets.

Clean up the stone and carry out a final examination of the entire series of crown facets which should be well-balanced and sharply cut with a smooth satin sheen on the unpolished faces.

Retain the last angle setting to commence the polishing phases, working in reverse order, girdle facets, star facets and finally the main facets. The correct angles for these should have been accurately recorded. Replace the cutting disc with a polishing lap and prepare a suitable polishing agent.

POLISHING THE CROWN FACETS

Charge the rotating lap with polish and lower the stone. Polish each girdle facet in turn in rotation, allowing the stone to remain on the lap for only a few seconds at a time. Inspect frequently, using a carefully directed light along the facet. Many machines have a flexible-arm lamp attached for this purpose.

Light to moderate pressure should be used, increasing slightly for larger facets. Do not over-polish as there is a risk of dragging material into the other facets and rounding off the sharpness of the ridges. This danger is increased if an oxide slurry is allowed to dry out on the lap, building up a concentration of dry powder on leading edges of the facets. Similarly, hardened particles of oxide may cause the facets to ride over the lap or even scratch the surface of the stone.

When the girdle facets are completed, reset the angle required for the star facets and polish as before. Follow by polishing the main facets at the recorded angles, which completes the crown. The stone is then cleaned thoroughly and made ready for transfer dopping to cut the pavilion facets.

PAVILION MAIN FACETS

The angle of the eight pavilion mains is a few degrees less than the crown mains and can be started at 43 degrees for quartz. Differences will occur in stones of varying sizes and proportions and final angles will be achieved through adjustments during cutting. Cut the facets in a similar sequence to the crown mains, commencing at 0/64 index, followed by 32 index and alternate between opposite pairs until all the facets meet at a point in a central position and form sharply cut ridges down the length.

By cutting each facet a little at a time the angles can be corrected as necessary. To attempt cutting a single facet the whole distance in one operation can be disastrous, leading to over-cutting the point and an off-centred pavilion, also to different thicknesses at the girdle. The broad ends of the main facets should stop short evenly, allowing a girdle thickness of about 2 per cent of the stone's width. Measurement in this case is largely a question of a practiced eye, but a razor-sharp girdle must be avoided to prevent chipping of the stone during setting. Further reduction in the girdle thickness must be allowed for when using two stages of cutting.

PAVILION GIRDLE FACETS

The sixteen girdle facets are positioned one at each side of the mains ridge and form elongated triangles with the base or spreading edge at the girdle and the points touching at the mains ridges about halfway down the pavilion.

Set the cutting angles a few degrees higher than the mains, about 45 degrees, and allow for progressive adjustments. Remember to record the correct angle. Cut adjacent pairs of facets a little at a time, carrying out constant inspections. Allow the facets to spread slowly at the girdle and creep along the ridge line. This control and matching appraisal is necessary to produce a cut gem of flawless symmetry.

POLISHING THE PAVILION FACETS

Do not alter the angle of the facetting arm. Remove the cutting lap, replacing with a polishing lap. Clean the stone carefully.

Polish all the girdle facets in rotation at the previous angle, observing the precautions and techniques outlined for polishing the crown facets. Change the angle to the pre-recorded mains angle and polish the series of main facets to complete the pavilion.

To polish the girdle, lower the arm to a position parallel to the lap (stone at right-angles, set 90 degrees). Release the index catch to allow free rotation of the facetting arm and polish the entire girdle. Remove the stone from the dop and clean thoroughly.

It should be noted that some cutters prefer to facet the girdle, giving an angular perimeter and a more clean-cut appearance to the stone. In some cases the point of the pavilion is also removed with a culet facet to make the termination less vulnerable to knocks.

The emerald cut

This particular cut is step-cut in a series of parallel facets on both crown and pavilion and is suited to coloured stones of every hue and intensity. Large stones cut in this way are enhanced by deep pavilions and increased rows of facets which produce a scintillating pattern of reflected light through the natural colouration of the

EMERALD CUT

cutting order, CROWN. 64 tooth gear

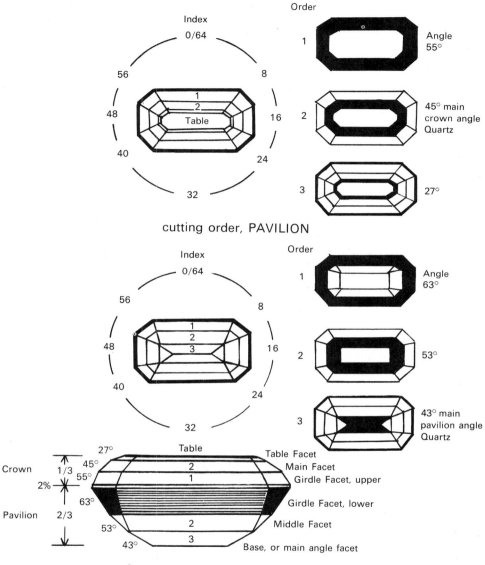

Order

Index

0/64

56   8

48   16

40   24

32

1   Angle 55°

2   45° main crown angle Quartz

3   27°

cutting order, PAVILION

Order

Index

0/64

56   8

48   16

40   24

32

1   Angle 63°

2   53°

3   43° main pavilion angle Quartz

Crown 1/3
27°
45°
55°
2%

Table Facet
Main Facet
Girdle Facet, upper
Girdle Facet, lower

Pavilion 2/3
63°
53°
43°

Middle Facet
Base, or main angle facet

Crown facets 1 and 2, approximately same height

Facet number 3 (next to table) half or less than mains

Pavilion facets – Girdle – approximate height of crown or
half height of pavilion
Middle and Base – half height of girdle facet

Figure 92. Emerald Cut: Diagram of cutting sequence

stone. The large parallel crown facets permit maximum entry of light for internal refraction and also reflect bands of light from the outer polished surfaces.

Cutting parallel facets requires some degree of expertise, and the sharp edges of the facet junctions must correspond along each side of the stone in continuous lines. Sometimes problems arise during polishing as uniformity of finish is not easy to achieve on large faces and slight variations not discernible at the cutting stages are clearly revealed on facet surfaces in the final polish. For example, if a facet edge is developing out of parallel the skilled cutter can spread the facet into place by using the cheater, by height adjustment or evenly increased pressure. These actions may change the angle of the face imperceptibly during cutting and must be precisely repeated at the polishing stage to mask the irregularity (figure 93).

BASIC FEATURES OF THE CUT

Depending on the size of stone, the crown can have two or three angled facets leading up to the horzontal plane of the table. Pavilion facets can number from three to six, or even more if the

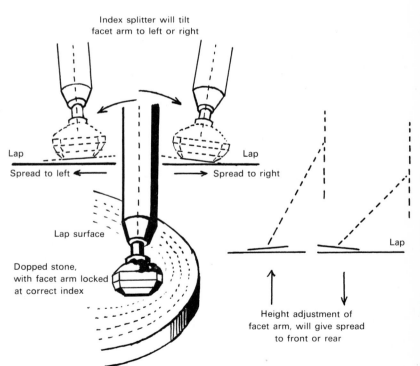

Figure 93. Index splitter (cheater) and height adjustment actions for spreading a polish or making minor alterations where needed

stone is deep enough, and the culet can terminate in either a sharp ridge or a fine culet facet.

The overall proportions of a stone are usually determined by the cutter, taking into account colour, size, number of facets and allowances for orientation, but angles for main facets must remain constant for particular minerals. Characteristic dimensions of the emerald cut include the crown or portion of stone above the girdle which can average one-third of the total height. Below the girdle the two-thirds pavilion depth is divided in horizontal bands stepping down to the culet. The first of these, next to the girdle, may be cut to half the total depth of the pavilion, the second facet may be half the depth of the girdle facet and subsequent facets are planned to suit the depth of the pavilion. Second and third facets are often of equal depth.

THE PRE-FORM

The emerald cut can utilize larger pieces of gem material and wastage is kept to a minimum by careful pre-forming. Examine the rough carefully and decide on a pre-form shape giving the most economical proportions for a finished stone. Irregular pieces of rough should be ground to remove sharp points and eliminate hollows as a preliminary to pre-forming. In this way a better assessment of the mass and possible shape can be made.

Avoid over-shaping and attempting to anticipate the facet angles. As the pre-form nears the desired proportions, allow a good outward curvature to the stone, both at crown and pavilion, giving a generous margin for the facet angles (figure 80). Corners can be lightly indicated to prevent sharp edges gouging the lap, if corner facets are required.

The completed pre-form can be dopped as previously outlined on page 91, with the girdle and pavilion areas clearly exposed for first cutting sequences.

SHAPING THE GIRDLE

Throughout each phase select the appropriate laps, according to preference, for either one or two stage cutting techniques with suitable abrasives and lubricants.

Secure the dopped stone in the chuck of the facetting arm and set the angle at 90 degrees. Lower the arm until the long side of the rectangular pre-form is in contact with the lap. Index at 0 or 64 (see index diagram figure 92) and grind the side perfectly flat. Turn the facetting arm and index 32 to place the opposite long side on the lap. Grind until flat and parallel to the other side. To grind the two ends, raise the facetting head a little, re-check the angle setting at 90 degrees, index and cut opposite ends succes-

105

sively at 16 followed by 48. Cut until ends are parallel and if square corners are intended continue until these are regular right-angles, otherwise the corners need not be sharply cut. If corner facets are required, which is more usual in an emerald cut, retain the angle setting at 90 degrees and cut the corners in rotations, matching the length of each cut. Index the corners at 8, 24, 40, 56.

CUTTING THE PAVILION

It should be noted that the principal angles mentioned for both crown and pavilion facets are based on angles most suitable for quartz. Angle variations for other gem materials are listed in appendix tables.

To cut the first series of pavilion facets, those bordering on the girdle, set the angle at 63 degrees, index 64 and adjust the height to place one of the long sides of the stone in contact with the lap and level with the squared-up girdle edge. Make any necessary adjustments.

Raise the stone from the lap prior to switching on the machine, then lower carefully and commence cutting. Spread the facet gradually down the stone and carry out frequent progress checks. Pay particular attention to the edge approaching the girdle and do not over-cut the portion needed to leave a two per cent girdle thickness in the completed stone. Cut the facet to approximately half the pavilion depth. Retaining the same height and angle, index the opposite long edge of the stone 32 and cut the next girdle facet.

Raise the head assembly for cutting the two opposite end facets, followed by the corner facets, ensuring a horizontal link-up of the eight facet edges around the stone.

Some cutters prefer to cut the long side facets and then cut the corners and ends in strict rotation, lining up the facets as work proceeds. The difficult point occurs when cutting the last girdle facet to match the rest in parallel continuity. Here the manipulation techniques of cheater and micro-adjustments can be employed to advantage to spread the facet edges into position. It is important to emphasize that facets are relatively small planes and that cutting is precision grinding. In some cases this requires only a touch on the lap, a close examination and a further fraction of a second on the lap to control the progress. Small stones and facets can be cut entirely with the fine grit in a single operation.

The second row of facets, eight in number, including the four corner facets, can be cut at 53 degrees, indexed as before. Gradually spread the facet depth to about half the depth of the girdle facet. Keep a constant check on parallel edges and be prepared to make any necessary adjustments. It will be seen that the corner facets are tapering towards the base at this stage and in some cases, depending on the proportions of the stone and number of facets, will terminate in triangles at either the second or third row with the inverted points touching the intersection of the main row of facets.

The third and final row of facets in a pavilion limited to three rows, will be the main facets and cut at 43 degrees for quartz. If the corner facets have been worked out, the main facets will probably number only four, two long and two short, intersecting in a sharp ridge. Index for the two sides and ends as before. Make sure the facets are running parallel and that the culet ridge is forming in a central position during cutting. This can be more easily controlled by cutting opposite sides a little at a time with frequent progress checks.

POLISHING THE PAVILION

Swing the facetting arm up and replace the cutting lap with a polishing disc. Retain the last cutting angle at 43 degrees and polish the main facets, working in reverse order towards the girdle and polishing each set of facets at the appropriate angles. Allow for any irregularities or adjustments made previously, which should have been recorded for reference. Complete the series of facets by polishing the girdle at 90 degrees.

Throughout the polishing operation inspect each facet carefully through a hand lens to check uniform progress; the entire row of facets should be examined before proceeding to the next angle change. Surface irregularities or slight misalignments of the facet junctions can often be corrected here by increased pressure on the facetting arm to spread the polish to required areas, although a repetition of cheater and height adjustments made previously may be necessary to produce a satisfactory polish.

Remove the dop from the chuck and prepare to reverse the stone by the transfer of dopping method outlined previously. When setting the stone in the new dop, test the long girdle edge with a horizontal plate to ensure the stone will rest flat on the lap at 90 degrees. Manipulation of the stone must be carried out before the wax begins to solidify. This is an essential alignment check for cutting parallel facets in both crown and pavilion on stones with straight-sided girdles.

CUTTING THE CROWN

Secure the dop in the facetting arm and lower to a horizontal position until the girdle is at 90 degrees with the long edge on the lap. Inspect closely for perfect horizontal contact and check the index reading at 64.

The height of the crown from girdle to table, approximately one-third of the total height of the stone, can now be established by cutting the table. Set the arm at 45 degrees and secure the stone and dop in the 45 degree angle adaptor. Lower the stone carefully to the lap and cut the table down to the required level. Repeat with the finer abrasive stage. Remember that this is a large and important surface and one of the more difficult facets to polish successfully. Cut the table to about two-thirds of the stone's total length. Follow immediately by polishing to satisfaction to complete the table.

Remove the 45 degrees adaptor and re-set the angle to cut the crown girdle facets at 55 degrees, indexing opposite sides at 64 followed by 32. Cut the ends and corners, linking up the facet ridges and ensuring a parallel thickness of the girdle which is now reduced to two per cent of the stone's depth.

Re-set the angle at 45 degrees and cut the eight main facets in the same cutting order as previously, bringing the girdle facet depth to approximately half the total height of the crown. At this stage the main facets may also have linked up to the table.

A third and final set of facets cut at a lower angle will reduce the size of the table and the depth of the main facet. The angle for the table facets will vary from about 27 degrees or less, according to the desired proportions of the table. In many cases the third facet is merely a narrow strip bordering the table and may be omitted in very small stones. When the table facet is cut to a depth of one-third of the main facet the overall reducing proportions of the crown facets will have a pleasing relationship.

Figures 94, 95. Stones cut from rock crystal mounted for display. Cut by Guy Wilson, Hull, England

Figure 96. Faceted ovoid cut by Dennis
Durham, Hull, England

POLISHING THE CROWN

The three remaining sets of crown facets are polished in reverse
order from the table facets, mains and, finally, the girdle facets.
Carry out a final inspection, remove the stone from the dop and
clean carefully.

Tumble polishing

Tumble polished stones are instantly recognizable by irregularity
of shape and absence of corners, edges and facets. The only approach to uniformity lies in the smoothness of surface and highly
polished finish on both concave and convex areas of the stones.
Mass production of polished stones by tumbling is largely a
mechanical process and apart from progress checks, grit changes,
and ensuring reasonable speeds, the operator has little direct
influence on the end product. Stones are sometimes shaped by
hand on a grinding wheel before tumbling; this speeds up the
action by eliminating early tumbling phases.

The tumbling operation is relatively simple and large quantities
of stones can be produced simultaneously inside a slowly revolving
drum or barrel. The action is similar to the movement of shingle

on a beach, rolled in the ebb and flow of successive tides, where sand acts as the abrasive agent. While transformation of rock fragments into smooth pebbles takes years through natural agencies, this is condensed into a matter of weeks in the tumbling process. If a careful selection is made of small beach pebbles which are already smooth and free from holes and fractures, this will save days of preliminary coarse grinding in the tumbler.

Tumbler barrels should be filled with stones and abrasive grit to approximately two-thirds capacity and water added to just cover the load. As far as possible all the stones should be of similar hardness. In the larger capacity drums all sizes of pebbles or rough rock up to $1\frac{1}{2}$-inches can be used but should be proportionately reduced for smaller tumblers. Stones should be inspected regularly to check progress during each grit run and at the end of each phase stones and barrel must be washed thoroughly before introducing finer grits or polish. During tumbling there is a weight loss in the total load due to abrasive action but this can be rectified by addition of fillers such as smooth pebbles to make up the bulk to the original loading. If correct weight loading is not maintained the tumbling action inside the barrel will be affected (figure 97).

Successful experiments have been carried out using the same slurry throughout the entire abrasive stages instead of washing

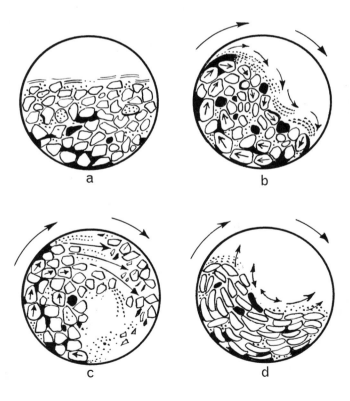

Figure 97. Tumbling action: (a) barrel loaded to two-thirds capacity; (b) correct tumbling speed will allow stones to cascade gently; (c) barrel revolving too fast will throw the contents resulting in broken and fractured stones; (d) barrel turning too slowly results in flattened stones

out when the grit size is changed. Fresh grits of finer grades are added when required. With this method, the slurry will be greatly thickened with worn grits and cutting debris, and the viscosity may need to be reduced by adding more water. Barrels and stones will still need a thorough washing before beginning the polishing phase. The accumulated sludge in the tumbler should be contained in polythene bags and deposited in a refuse bin, and *not* poured down the household drainage system.

At this point it should be stressed that no hard and fast rules can be laid down on tumbling procedures; satisfactory results are the outcome of understanding the basic processes, followed by personal experiment and discovery. Tumbling speeds are recommended by manufacturers to ensure correct usage of their machines and are governed by such things as design of the unit, shape and capacity of tumbler barrels (figure 98). Length of tumbling time, quantities of abrasives and grit sizes used are all variable factors and the following suggestions are intended as a general guide only.

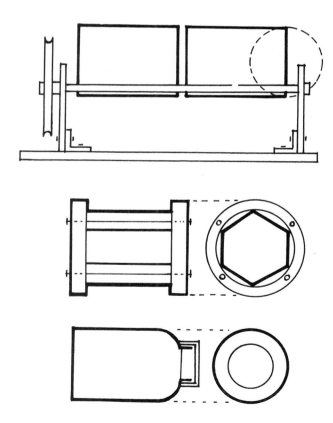

Figure 98. Types of tumbler barrels

Tumbling phases

The most widely used procedure involves three abrasive stages, one polishing stage and a final rinse. Silicon carbide grits in varying grades from coarse to fine are used in the wearing down stages and final polishing is carried out with tin oxide or cerium oxide.

Phase One: 80 or 120 grit size, 2 oz for each 1 lb of stones
Four to ten days continuous running

Phase Two: 220 or 320 grit, 1 oz for each 1 lb of stones
Four to seven days continuous running

Phase Three: 400 or 500 grit, 1 oz for each 1 lb of stones
Four to seven days continuous running

For very smooth water-worn pebbles only two abrasive stages may be necessary; 220 grit for up to ten days, followed by 400 or 500 grit for up to seven days.

Sharp, angular stones and hammered rough rock may take up to three weeks of continuous running with 80 grit in the first stage to wear down the stones to reasonable shapes. Remember to make frequent progress checks.

Polishing Phase: Cerium or tin oxide, approximately $\frac{1}{2}$ oz to 1 lb of stones. Add plastic granules or other fillers. Run for three days or until satisfactory polish is achieved.

Final Rinse: Run for 12 hours with water and a little detergent powder. Add plastic granules to cushion the load.

Vibratory tumblers

The hoppers or containers, usually cast in light metal alloy with thick polyvinyl lining, remain in fixed position instead of tumbling in the accepted sense (figure 99). The stones are subjected to high-speed vibrations, producing rapid agitation of the load, and in addition there is gradual rotation of the whole mass within the container. The complete grinding and polishing cycle is speeded up during the vibratory process and a batch of stones can be finished in two to five days – depending on their composition and original surface condition – compared with two to three weeks in a rotary tumbler. During operation the rate of vibrations can be in excess of 2500 per minute and the load, with abrasive charge, remains in a state of suspension, supported in a thickened solution containing minimum moisture. In this form, the stones are evenly coated with abrasive emulsion and, as the viscosity reduces the impact of stones against each other, it is possible to process material of different hardnesses at the same time with minimum weight loss or danger of fracturing.

Prepare a load which is evenly balanced in variable sizes of stones and proportion of rock types, ensuring that up to 25 per

Plate 3. Snuff box. Citrine surrounded by agates, pearls, aquamarine, amethyst, garnet and amazonite

(Crown copyright. Reproduced by permission of the Institute of Geological Sciences)

Figure 99. Vibratory tumbler with twin hoppers. Viking Vibra-sonic VT 12 Geode Industries, New London, Iowa, USA

cent consists of smaller stones, three-quarters to half an inch, to fill up spaces between the larger stones. The load should occupy about 80 per cent of the total capacity of the container and the weight of stones should be recorded, together with amounts of abrasive and water added. A low moisture content assists in the abrasive and polishing actions and chemical additives in tablet form to act as emulsifying or water thickening agents will give a slippery quality to the batter-like mixture. Other thickening materials can be used, such as ground rice powder or dehydrated potato powder, and a suitable consistency arrived at by trial and error. More thickening agent should be used when polishing soft or easily fractured stones. Inspection of the load should be carried out at approximately eight-hourly intervals and if the mixture has thickened to a viscous sludge from accumulated grinding waste then it will be necessary to add water sparingly.

Two or three grit phases can be used and the stones and containers must be washed thoroughly between grit changes to prevent any danger of grit contamination. Ideally, a separate hopper should be kept exclusively for the final polishing stage. During the pre-polish and final polish additives such as plastic granules, vermiculite or crushed nut shells are used as filling material to cushion the stones. The quantities of grit, polish and water used at each stage are not given here since manufacturers of vibratory tumblers supply details of amounts recommended specifically for their machines. It is advisable to record carefully such factors as load weights, stone varieties, quantities of grit and water, for future reference and comparison of results.

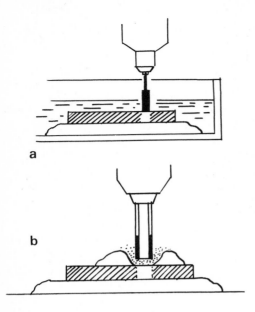

Figure 100. Methods of drilling holes in stones: (a) Drilling with diamond-tipped drill; (b) using a tube drill with abrasive grits

Drilling holes in stones

Several methods can be employed to drill holes in stones. Some are laborious, requiring time and patience as in the case of primitive bow drills or metal tube and grit drills, but much will depend on the hardness of materials. Speedier and more precise drilling techniques are possible with diamond abrasives.

Holes can be made in soft stones with hand drills and flexible drive shafts fitted to power drills using fine metal burrs and twist drills, but many of the stones cut by amateur lapidaries border on the harder quartz range and can be drilled only by gradual abrasion administered by loose abrasive grits and hollow metal tubes or diamond tipped drills. These can either be electrically powered or battery-operated.

To use a tube drill, make a small enclosure or dam of plasticine or modelling clay centred round the position of the hole. For convenience, the stone can be held in position by dopping it to a flat piece of wood. As the tube is rotating, at speeds up to 2000 rev/min, a slurry of silicon carbide grit and water is fed to the tip and is contained in the well of plasticine. Although slow and tedious this method is effective. (Figure 100b).

Diamond tipped drills reach maximum efficiency operating at high speeds, approximately 4000 to 5000 rev/min, and require constant coolant supply. One method of ensuring adequate coolant is to press the stone into a small piece of plasticine in the bottom of a shallow dish and cover it with water. As drilling takes place the water will also wash away cutting debris from the diamond points (figure 100a).

In all drilling operations the pressure on the drill must be reduced at regular intervals to assist the cleansing of the drill tip and, in the case of loose abrasives, redistribute the grits under the drill tube. Care must be taken to prevent the drill breaking through the stone too rapidly at the end of the cut as this may cause material to flake off underneath. It may be necessary to reverse the stone and drill from the other side until the holes meet, particularly when drilling beads.

For drilling holes of larger dimensions, hollowing out bowls and vases, or cutting rings of different thicknesses from rock slabs, core drills of various diameters are used. These consist of hollow core tubes or double-ringed tips impregnated with diamond or used with loose particles of abrasive. The tubes are secured in the chuck of a drill press and the work firmly supported on the drilling table. Cutting is done by abrasion and must never be forced by excessive pressure. Ease the drill upwards frequently and ensure adequate coolant supply.

7 Treatment of
Particular Stones

In cutting awkward minerals which never seem to progress beyond the sanding stages the problem may be in the stone itself or in the method of working. Perhaps the fault lies in the fact that the earlier sanding stages have not been thoroughly carried out and this should be checked by examining the stone through a magnifying lens before making any further attempt at polishing. The choice of lap and polishing medium can often affect the final result and after persisting for a time without achieving a satisfactory polish a different approach should be tried. Many of the stones requiring special treatment for a good finish occur in the lower hardness range or contain quantities of softer minerals in their composition.

Stones requiring special techniques

Quartz varieties are on the whole very responsive to standard lapidary procedures and, apart from the necessity to avoid over-heating, present few problems. Exceptions include moss agate, where dendritic inclusions break through the surface and small cavities appear very pronounced when filled with polishing oxides. In most cases careful sanding in the early stages will seal the imperfections but the cutter must be prepared to return frequently to sanding with fine abrasives and using adequate water coolant. A similar difficulty can arise with very fibrous tiger-eye, and when cutting cabochons correct orientation of the material will prevent ends of coarse fibres appearing on the surface of the dome.

Jasper, composed of silica infused with coloured clays and sometimes with metallic mineral inclusions, is susceptible to undercutting. This often occurs at the polishing stage when a felt disc is used and is caused by friction and heat. A leather disc and cerium oxide gives greatly improved results.

Chalcedony of uniform composition, such as carnelian, is sensitive to over-heating and to vibration from rough grinding on unevenly worn wheels. The molecular cohesion of the material can be upset by harsh treatment and result in minute fractures or splitting of the stone. Caution should be exercised when re-cutting a stone to change either the shape or proportion for a new setting. It will have already undergone changes during earlier cutting and will be in a brittle state so that a higher rate of fracturing can be expected.

The following short list of stones which are frequently a source of frustration during cutting or polishing are arranged in order of decreasing hardness. The suggested techniques are primarily concerned with cutting cabochons or flat sections using silicon carbide but many of the problems can be simplified by using diamond abrasives.

Treatment of particular stones

JADE Jadeite H $6\frac{1}{2}$–7. Nephrite H 6–$6\frac{1}{2}$

When working with jade problems of finish become more pronounced during sanding and polishing and the surface of the stone is subject to roughness and orange-skin texture. The basis of a good polish starts with meticulous sanding on a 220 grit silicon carbide wet/dry surface with copious water coolant, and continuing on a 400 grade. The stone must not be allowed to overheat or drag on a dry sanding surface at this stage. The vital sanding is done on a well-worn sanding disc of 600 grade employing the following technique: sand with the surface wet for a short period, using moderate pressure; gradually allow the disc to become dry and, at the same time increase the pressure on the stone until a smooth glazing occurs. This action can be repeated if necessary, starting wet. Complete the final polishing on a soft leather polishing lap using a slurry of oxide and water, preferably chrome oxide for best results.

FELDSPAR H 6–$6\frac{1}{2}$. Amazonite, Labradorite, Moonstone, Sunstone.

Selection of good material and careful orientation is most important for success with feldspars. The pronounced cleavage demands extra care and stones should not be subjected to harsh vibration from coarse-grained grinding wheels. Slower grinding speeds can be used to advantage and a constant supply of water must be used at each stage of grinding and sanding, which must be done gradually with gentle pressures. Pre-polish on a fine grade, well-worn sanding disc and complete the polishing on felt with cerium oxide.

The beauty of these stones lies in the colour and reflected glow of light (Schiller effect) when viewed from different angles. Orientation of these qualities within a cabochon dome must be carefully considered prior to cutting. By wetting the stone and allowing a direct, overhead light to fall on the surface in different positions the maximum display of schiller can be determined and retained in the same manner as cutting proceeds. Check repeatedly and be prepared to modify the cabochon in the early stages as required, for example by re-positioning the centre of the dome or lowering the height. A moonstone can thus be oriented to produce a play of light either as a central spot or an elongated band.

LAPIS LAZULI H $5\frac{1}{2}$

Lapis never attains a mirror polish, producing only a matt sheen which intensifies the blue ground and contrasts with golden flecks of pyrites present in good quality rough. Comparatively a soft material, it requires careful shaping followed by wet sanding, using gentle pressures in the early stages. Final sanding is carried out on a 600 grit disc. Avoid excessive heat and polish on soft leather with a paste of tin or chrome oxide. Undercutting is likely to occur in white or grey areas abundant in poor quality lapis, giving uneven qualities of finish.

OPAL H $5\frac{1}{2}$

Hydrated silica, very absorbent and dependent on moisture for perfect conditioning. It is vulnerable to dehydration through over-heating, which places the material in a critical and brittle condition. Make sure the stone is kept wet during each cutting and sanding stage. Trimming can be done with a thin diamond blade but owing to porosity water coolant should be used.

Grind and shape on a 220 grit wheel running at motor speed for control of cutting rate. Delicacy in handling and lightness of touch is essential as the rate of abrasion is rapid. Sand on 220 grade disc followed by refinements on a worn 400 or 600 grit disc as a pre-polishing phase, using liberal water coolant. Polish on leather with cerium oxide.

OBSIDIAN H 5

Frustrations with this material occur not in the finishing stages but during the preparatory grinding and shaping since it is brittle and will chip and flake if ground too hard or allowed to overheat. Sanding up to 400 grit stage should be done wet, followed by polishing on felt with cerium oxide.

FLUORSPAR variety Blue John H4

Care must be taken during grinding and shaping to prevent crumbling and disturbing the crystalline structure. Before sawing or grinding the stone should be immersed in melted pale lemon resin, maintaining the heat to keep it in a liquid state. This enables the resin to seep into the material as a binding and waterproofing agent. It would be misleading to give an exact length of time for this heat treatment but if continued too long the lighter parts of the crystalline zoning which is a feature of Blue John becomes stained from yellow to brown.

After removal from the resin and when thoroughly cool, the stone can be sawn and then shaped carefully on a 220 grit wheel, using water as required to prevent overheating. In the final sanding stages smooth away all traces of surface resin. A leather lap used with tin oxide is suitable for polishing.

RHODOCHROSITE H 4

Structurally weak along the banded pattern lines and highly susceptible to knocks and overheating. Gentle treatment is needed because of softness and grinding should be done on the finer grade of wheel at half the normal grinding speed. Sand wet on previously used discs up to 600 grade as new discs are rather harsh and remove material too rapidly. Polish on leather with tin oxide.

Absorbent; use water coolant instead of oil for sawing.

MALACHITE H $3\frac{1}{2}$–4

Absorbent material which should be sawn with water rather than oil to retain brightness of colour. Grind gently on finer wheels with liberal water coolant and sand wet on 400 to 600 grit discs. Avoid inhaling malachite dust which is poisonous; never cut dry. A slurry of chrome oxide, to which may be added a few drops of vinegar, is used on a leather polishing lap. Cerium oxide may be used as an alternative polishing medium. A final rub by hand on a soft leather pad with a mixture of polishing oxide and detergent can be advantageous.

SERPENTINE VARIETIES H 2–4

Prone to undercutting and absorbent. For sawing, water is preferable to oil to prevent dullness. Grind and sand carefully with water coolant in the earlier stages and polish on leather with chrome or cerium oxide. Frictional heat is the cause of roughness and pitting of the stone's surface and polishing on felt should be avoided. If final polishing results are unsatisfactory by usual methods, return to a well-worn 600 grit sanding disc and start sanding wet. Gradually allow the disc to dry out, applying more pressure on the stone. A good surface should result and it may not be necessary to polish further. A rub by hand on a soft cloth with a few drops of light oil applied to the stone will impart additional lustre.

Techniques so far discussed for polishing different minerals have been proved successful by many lapidaries. The choice of polishing medium such as cerium, tin or chrome oxides is largely a question of preference and although chrome oxide has been recommended as a superior medium for some stones it is messy to use and for this reason is often avoided. Pre-polishing agents, some of which are aluminium oxide derivatives, are manufactured under various trade names and frequently used on either felt or leather laps to prepare the stone's surface for the final polish.

ORGANIC MATERIALS

Jet, H $3\frac{1}{2}$ and **amber** H $2\frac{1}{2}$ are gem materials of organic origins and require special care when working with powered equipment but rapidly acquire a high polish. Both are tough, compact materials but owing to softness, grinding and shaping is rapid and should be carried out on either a 220 grit wheel or 220 grit wet/dry disc. Water coolant is essential despite the build-up of brown slurry when cutting jet. Both materials are heat sensitive but adequate coolant will prevent burning and formation of crackled surfaces. A smooth pre-polish can be achieved on a 400 sanding disc followed by a well-worn 600 grit disc. At this stage, sand wet at the start and finally allow the disc to run dry. Should further polishing be necessary, use a soft leather lap with cerium oxide or rub by hand on velvet or chamois leather.

Kauri gum from New Zealand, though not a form of amber is one of the hardened resin substitutes with many of the qualities of amber. Cutting and polishing techniques are very similar but the material tends to become tacky if frictional heat is not controlled.

ABALONE SHELL

This attractive Mexican shell, as well as Paua shell from New Zealand, is widely used as a decorative jewellery material. It is not difficult to cut but the specialized treatment during preparation is worth mentioning here.

Removal of the rough outer shell layers can be accomplished by filing or by coating with dilute nitric acid solution and washing away the dissolved layers. Prior to rinsing with clear water, the acid can be neutralized with ammonia to prevent further reaction on the shell. It is recommended that this treatment is done in the open air or in a well ventilated room. Rubber gloves will protect hands from contact with acid. During rough filing a face mask with a filter pad should be worn to prevent inhalation of dust particles.

Shells can be worked easily with simple tools such as hacksaws and files. Sanding can be done by hand and polished by rubbing vigorously on a soft cloth pad with cerium oxide. Hand methods are favoured by many when cutting shells but powered equipment can be used. It is important to use liberal water coolant when grinding and sanding to counteract nauseous dust and fumes characteristic of this material.

CATS-EYE AND STAR STONES

Minerals with fibrous inclusions orientated in a particular way will reflect a silky sheen known as chatoyancy. Cats-eye stones cut and polished as cabochons display a single band of moving light at right angles to the horizontal formation of the fibres (figure 101). For correct orientation the base of the cabochon must lay parallel to the fibres and the direction of the chatoyant streak calculated to run with the longer dimension in an oval shaped stone. By adjust-

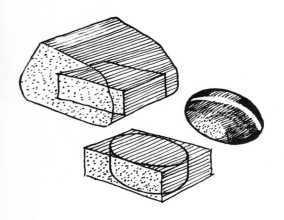

Figure 101. Correct orientation of cats-eye cabochons

Figure 102. Orientation of Tigers-eye: (a) Slabs cut parallel to moving bands of light; (b) in good quality rough, light bands will be at right-angles to straight fibres; (c) different cabochon positions to give elongated, diagonal or short bands; (d) single bands of light isolated to give cats-eye effect; wide in shallow dome, narrow in high dome; (e) orientation of cabochons if fibres not at right-angles to edge of slab

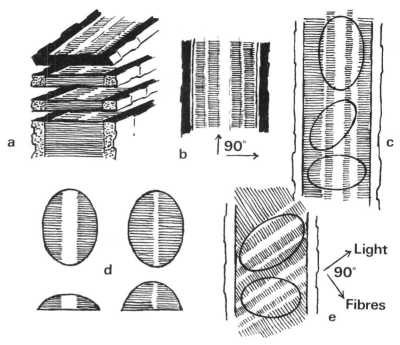

ing the height of the cabochon the reflected cats-eye can be broad in a shallow dome or narrowed to a thin line in a high ridged dome. In order to centre a single cats-eye with any degree of success the fibrous inclusions within the gem rough must be perfectly straight. Any warping of the fibres will cause distortion of the reflected light.

In sharp contrast, other chatoyant stones show a very pronounced fibrous structure, often twisted and irregular, particularly in the popular quartz gem tiger's-eye. The structure of this material produces multiple light bands which move across the surface of the stone when viewed from different angles. It is also possible to cut single cats-eye gems from tiger's-eye (figure 102).

Qualities of asterism in crystalline gem material can be seen to advantage when cut and polished in hemispherical form or high-domed cabochons. In shallow cut cabochons the star may disappear towards the edges. Good star formations depend on the concentration of reflective fibres within the crystalized structure running parallel to the crystal faces. The radial spread of the star conforms to the symmetry of the particular crystal system, for example in four to six directions and considerably more in the case of duplicate structural growths or twinning. Correctly orientated spheres will show a star at opposite poles. The horizontal base of a star cabochon is formed at right angles to the C axis (figure 104). Stars found in synthetic gem materials are often more sharply defined.

Figure 103. Perfect example of asterism in a blue star sapphire. Collection of John F. Turner, Wakefield, England

Figure 104. Orientation of star stones

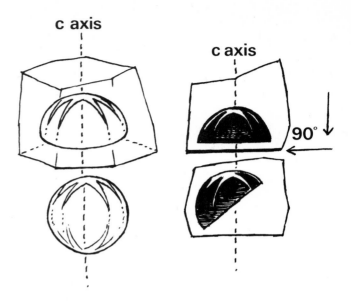

Orientation. Locating the star is a simple matter if the rough crystal is complete or some of the crystal faces are present to determine the *C* axis. Difficulties arise however where the shape of the gem rough is entirely irregular in outline. Minerals which reveal asterism can be semi-transparent or translucent, with pale to deep colouration. In many cases the fibrous structure or inclusions responsible for asterism will not be visible to the naked eye. By careful abrasion all points and hollows should be removed and a smooth surface establish over the entire stone to a satin finish. Polishing will produce even better results and in some cases tumble polishing can assist the discovery of a star or cats-eye. Wet the stone or smear with refined oil, which remains on the surface longer, and illuminate with a single pin-point of light directly over the stone. Move the stone about until a positive circle of light is established in one position, denoting the centre of the star. In some cases star rays will be visible in the curvature of the stone. Mark the position of the central spot of light or intersecting of the light bands, which will be the top of the cabochon dome. Cut the dome to the required proportions and level off the base. Round high-domed cabochons will reflect a well-balanced star, while oval-shaped stones will elongate the star rays in one direction. Sand and polish, carrying out repeated checks for orientation with the overhead light source and be prepared to make minor adjustments during shaping. Often a star becomes more evident when the cabochon is placed on the surface of a mirror and light is strongly reflected back through the stone. For this reason, star stones are sometimes enhanced by having a reflective surface applied to the base, for example metallic foil.

The procedure for locating a cats-eye is almost identical but the fibrous structure is often more evident and the chatoyant band well-defined when the stone is moved under a light. By observing the structural pattern the position and shape of the cabochon base can be quickly determined once the cats-eye has been centred. Many of these stones are opaque or slightly translucent.

Cat's-eye stones	*Star stones*
chrysoberyl	sapphire
quartz	ruby
tourmaline	rose quartz
tiger's-eye (crocidolite)	garnet
	diopside

Making an opal doublet

Opal can be obtained of a thickness suitable for cutting cabochons or as thin seams and layers. Quite often the purchase of an assortment of opal chips will yield not only material for small cabochons but also thin flakes with good colour which can be used for the upper layers of doublets. As opal is sold by weight and valued by presence of colour or 'fire' the cutter must avoid wastage.

Thin seams of precious opal are found in a matrix of sandstone and associated with an opaque grey 'potch'. In order to determine the amount of opal which can be utilized it is necessary to remove the matrix and grind a flat surface on the exposed opal layer. If a workable diameter with a reasonable amount of fire remains, it will be possible to prepare a thin slice for a doublet either by slicing with a fine trim-saw or by grinding to the required thickness. In the case of a trimmed slice from a larger piece of solid opal the preparation will be simplified and it will only be necessary to examine the material for suitable colour orientation.

DOUBLET BACKING

Material used for the base or backing of a doublet should be of approximately the same hardness as opal to allow a similar rate of cutting. Black obsidian and black glass, having compact structure and uniform intensity, are very suitable for the purpose but careful grinding is essential because of their brittle nature. Inferior pieces of opal and dark grey opal 'potch' can also be used as a backing for doublets. Cement for bonding the precious opal to a backing can be one of the cold resin adhesives or shellac and a black colouring agent can be added. The dark background strengthens the colour and in some cases gives the appearance of black opal.

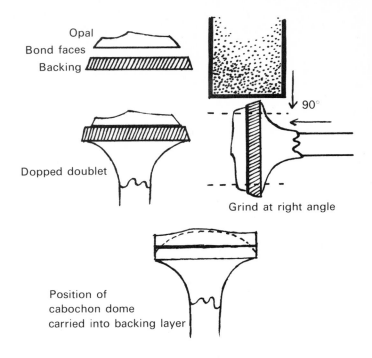

Figure 105. Stages in cutting a doublet

Opal
Bond faces
Backing

Dopped doublet

90°

Grind at right angle

Position of
cabochon dome
carried into backing layer

PROGRESSIVE STAGES (figure 105)

Select and orientate a piece of precious opal for the upper part of the doublet and grind a perfectly flat face on the area to be bonded. Grind carefully on a 220 grit wheel with plenty of water coolant or use loose grits on plate glass. Small opal chips will need to be dopped before grinding.

Grind a corresponding flat face on a dopped slice of backing material which should be slightly wider than the opal. Remove both stones from dopsticks and clean thoroughly.

Apply a thin coating of adhesive to both flat surfaces and make contact by sliding together to make a perfect bond free from air pockets. If using melted shellac the stones should be warmed, but avoid overheating. Allow to set thoroughly.

Re-dop the doublet with opal uppermost. When set, hold the dopstick at right-angles to the front of a 220 grit wheel which should be revolving at the slower machine speed. Turn the stick slowly, grinding the perimeter of the stone to shape and using plenty of water coolant. Inspect frequently and continue grinding until all points are removed and the cemented joint conforms to the size and shape required. Leave the stone dopped for the next stage.

Decide on the profile shape of the precious opal. There may be enough material to cut a shallow cabochon or the opal flake

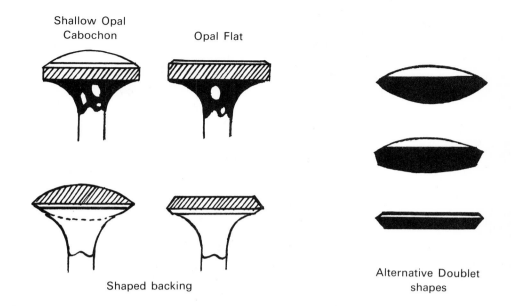

Shallow Opal Cabochon

Opal Flat

Shaped backing

Alternative Doublet shapes

Figure 106. Doublet profiles

may only allow for a flat-topped stone (figure 106). Using the 220 wheel, running at motor speed, apply gentle pressure to grind the desired shape. Carry the edges of the cabochon dome into the backing layer, bringing the doublet girdle below the cement line. With a flat-top, cut a bevel around the edge to expose the black backing. By doing this the whole of the opal will be exposed in a jewellery setting and the thin black edging provides a contrasting feature. A more important reason for carrying the girdle below the bonded joint is to prevent any damage to the opal during setting. Do not sand and polish at this stage in case later modifications are needed.

Remove from dopstick and re-dop on the reverse side. The backing material can now be shaped as an inverted cabochon or with a level base. Avoid creating a sharp edge on the girdle during grinding as this would crumble when setting. If a high finish is desired the base can be sanded and polished at this stage.

To complete the doublet, reverse the dopping once more and sand the opal on a 400 or 600 wet/dry disc, using water coolant to prevent dehydration of the stone. Polish with a slurry of cerium or tin oxide on a felt disc run at slowest speed. Remove from dopstick and clean up the doublet.

An opal triplet

Cutting triple-layered stones with a thin centre flake of opal surmounted by transparent quartz is widely practised. The triplet

Figure 107. An opal triplet

Clear quartz (Rock crystal)

Thin opal flake

Backing

is worked in a similar way to the doublet but usually cut as cabochons with the dark material forming a flat base layer supporting the opal veneer. The piece of rock crystal is cemented to the opal with a thin film of colourless adhesive, then domed to the required shape. The polished quartz dome provides excellent protection for the precious opal and the curvature of the transparent material magnifies the play of colour and suggests greater depth (figure 107).

8 Making Ornamental Objects

Carving

Lapidaries desiring a change from cutting cabochons and the rigid disciplines of facetting often find a freer and more creative outlet for their skills in one of the various forms of carving. The reluctance to embark on what are regarded as specialized arts is understandable but the amateur lapidary is free to pursue these crafts at his own level and has the advantage of previous attainments and acquired knowledge of cutting techniques. Realization that gemstone carving is a gradual abrasive process in much the same way as other forms of gem-cutting will provide the necessary confidence to take the first steps. Skill will be acquired through repeated practice and critical appraisal of completed works.

Many cutters will already possess equipment such as saws, grinders, drills and even small lathes which can be used or modified for carving projects. Cutting tools and abrasives will depend on the hardness of gem material and type of work involved. Diamond drills, burrs and a whole range of diamond impregnated discs and carving points will provide the most effective service and can be used in power drills, flexible drive attachments and belt-driven shafts but battery-operated hand drills can also be employed. Small tools can be easily made to suit a particular purpose and used with an applied slurry of silicon carbide grits (figure 108).

Figure 108. Examples of home-made carving tools which will fit in a drill chuck: (a) types of bolts used; (b) bolt head sawn off to fit into drill chuck; (c) single or multiple washers added to screw end secured by nut, used with abrasive slurries; (d) round-headed bolt used with grits for hollowing out

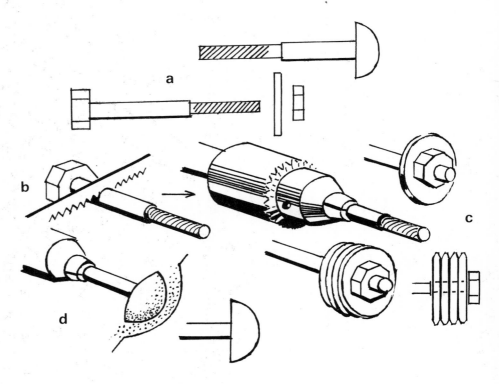

Softer stones may be worked without powered equipment and a collection of coarse rasps, files, a hacksaw and engraving tools are adequate.

Where possible, work in a well ventilated room to counteract problems of dust, which can be troublesome with some stones. A filter-pad breathing mask is recommended when carving or turning, or ideally, machines should be situated close to an extractor fan. The use of old vacuum cleaners with hoses fixed at strategic points can be advantageous for dust extraction. Many of the difficulties can be minimized by applying water coolants and rinsing the stones frequently.

Carving in the round

Working 'in the round' offers many advantages over other forms of gemstone carving since work can be viewed from every angle and readily handled for cutting in any direction. Removal of stock is more rapid in the roughing-out stages through ease of manipulation against powered cutting tools, also a broader concept of shape and mass is possible in three-dimensions.

Stone by its very nature calls for simplification in design of basic forms, particularly where resistance to abrasion increases with the harder gem materials. This imposed restraint will prove a blessing to those who may be tempted to adorn their carvings with irrelevant details (figure 109). When designing, free-standing

Figure 109. Bird form carved in verdite. Collection of John F. Turner, Glenjoy Lapidary Supplies, Wakefield, England

sculptures any slender projections and delicate supports which would be vulnerable to knocks and breakage should be avoided. Stone is brittle when reduced to spindle-like proportions and design features of this kind are better exploited in relief carvings where backgrounds provide linking supports.

Close observation of essential lines and structure in natural forms will lead to a design approach more suited to the materials, and a personal sketchbook or scrapbook of ideas from all sources will prove helpful. Reference to examples of small carvings and sculptures produced by craftsmen in older cultures often reveals astonishing perception of form and purity of line.

The desire for realism in portraying popular objects such as animals, birds and the human figure may prove a source of frustration to many when attempting carved objects for the first time because of a limited knowledge of form or artistic judgement and uncoordinated technical skills. In order to gain familiarity with tools and materials and acquire a feeling for spatial design, unhampered by subject conformity, an abstract or non-pictorial

Figure 110. Abstract form in soapstone

approach is recommended. Using hand or powered tools, carving by intuition and developing natural features and shapes assessed in different lights, original forms will gradually emerge from the rough piece of stone (figures 110, 111). In a creative exercise of this kind technical problems can be solved through lowering portions of the stone to different levels with contrasting curved and angular surfaces, by piercing holes and by the removal of areas to create new spaces. Different surface finishes can be explored by sanding, polishing and texturing with a variety of tools.

Figure 111. Curved form with pierced hole in alabaster

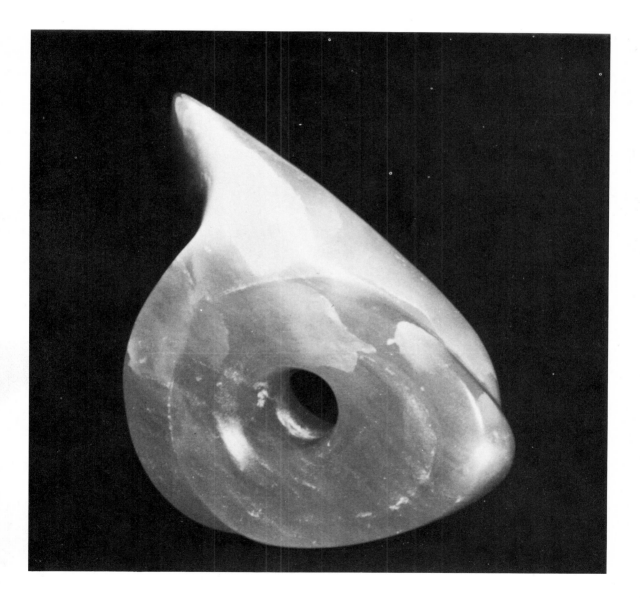

Figure 112. Rough piece of green bowenite which suggested a frog shape

Figure 113. Carving frog shape using metal rasp in flexible drive

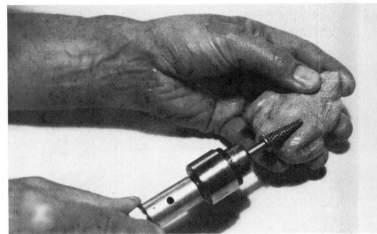

Figure 114. Stages in carving a small animal in alabaster: (Left) Form marked out on block; (Right) Block sawn to rough outline

Figure 115. (Left) Rough shaping to basic form; (Right) Contours smoothed with finer abrasives

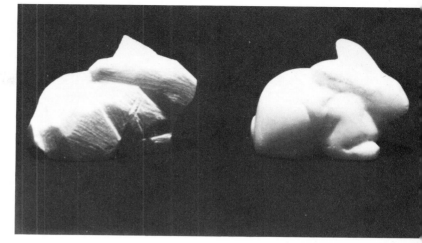

Figure 116. Polishing, using felt mop in battery-operated drill

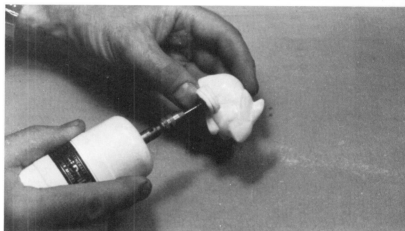

Figure 117. Completed carving

Figure 118. Angel fish carved in Brazilian agate, mounted on bed of natural quartz crystals. Collection of John F. Turner, Glenjoy Lapidary Supplies, Wakefield, England

Carving in relief

Relief carving is one of the more exacting forms of lapidary art and unlike work 'in the round' cannot be turned and evaluated from many different viewpoints. The height of relief, or projection from the background, will vary according to subject, scale and individual preference for high or low relief (figure 119). It is important to remember that the direction of lighting influences the form and total appearance of a relief and the darker shadows from one source will become light when the work is moved. This aspect of relief carving should be used to advantage during cutting by repeated changes of position and viewing under different lights. However, there may be instances where the work has been designed for viewing in one place with a single directional light and in these cases cutting must be done under similar lighting conditions.

Depending on personal interests, subjects can be totally abstract or based on the human form, animals, flowers etc, and presented

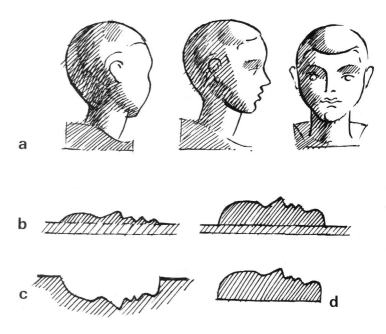

Figure 119. Different forms of carving: (a) carving in the round; (b) high and low relief; (c) intaglio; (d) relief cut-out

a

b

c

d

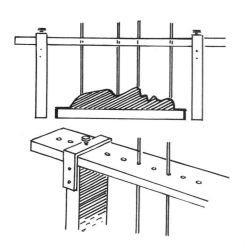

Figure 120. Aid for checking relative heights when working from a maquette

in either a realistic or decorative manner. A certain amount of stylization of form is desirable for the particular medium and unnecessary details should be omitted in order to simplify the finishing processes. Consideration must be given to the overall design and relationship between the carved forms and their arrangement on the background area. A realistic height for the proposed subject must be allowed for when choosing a suitable piece of stone and any natural banding or pattern used to advantage. Sometimes markings on the stone will suggest a possible subject.

Carefully prepared sketches or working drawings showing a plan and two elevation viewpoints will be helpful. A full-scale maquette modelled in clay, wax or a firm-setting modelling compound can be made prior to working on the stone. In this way an approximation of the basic shapes and form can be established without the dangers of over-cutting in the harder materials. It must be remembered throughout the carving that any part of the stone removed is final and cannot be replaced. When carving from a model the use of dividers or small calipers will greatly assist in transferring the exact proportions to the stone and serve as a progress check. A simply constructed aid for checking relative heights is illustrated in the diagram (figure 120).

Carving should proceed gradually, only the broad planes reduced to required levels at the start, and no attempt should be made at detailed cutting. When the various levels are established as a whole, details can be introduced and later refined, adding also surface textures and other decorative embellishments to the basic forms. Levelled background areas can be smooth or textured and either polished or left in a rough state to form a sharp contrast with the raised portions.

Liveliness of outline or varied edge treatment at the junction of relief and ground areas can make all the difference between a dull, insensitive carving and a vital, expressive piece of work. This fluidity of line, carried through to the internal surface of the design, adds to essential rhythms and movement in appropriate subjects.

When carving for the first time it is advisable to start on very soft stones such as alabaster (gypsum) and soapstone (talc) to gain control of tools and develop an understanding of simple forms. These soft stones can be worked entirely by hand with simple scrapers, knives, an assortment of files and hacksaw-blades. Files and rasps tend to overload with powdered debris during cutting, which prevents effective use, and this can be remedied by periodically tapping the file gently or cleaning out the grooves with a stiff wire brush.

Marks left on the stone after gouging and scraping can be removed by use of various grades of wet/dry silicon carbide paper cut or torn to requirements and either held in the fingers or wrapped and glued to small sticks shaped into points and wedges for difficult corners. Application of water to the work will assist the smoothing process and prevent the spread of dust but accumulated sludge obscures the design and needs to be sponged away from time to time.

Polish with tin oxide or cerium oxide slurry on cloth or soft leather and finally rub over vigorously with a piece of velvet. In some instances the merest film of light oil can be rubbed into the surface to intensify the sheen on the highlighted portions of the carving.

When working the harder gem minerals powered saws and abrasion in the form of belt-driven discs, points and drills may be necessary, using silicon carbide, aluminium oxide or diamond. Many of the abrasive tools can be made by the cutter to meet particular situations; alternatively a range of manufactured small tools is available for mounting in a flexible drive chuck or battery-operated hand engravers. Where small lathes and powered shafts are used cutting speeds must be geared to allow adequate control of the tool and work-piece. Coolant fluids and intermittent working will guard against overheating.

RELIEF CARVING FOR JEWELLERY

Stones in higher hardness groups or those of tough, compact materials are found to be more suited to carving small decorative

Plate 4. Opal group. Rough opal and cut stones including a carved opal and faceted fire opals

(Crown copyright. Reproduced by permission of the Institute of Geological Sciences)

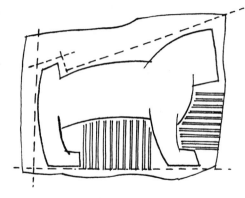

Figure 121. Making parallel saw-cuts to remove unwanted portions

motifs for brooches and pendants than those of soft, friable nature.

To prepare small pieces for carving, slab and trim the rough to required proportions on a diamond saw and level off both sides of the blank. Make a template of the design motif by cutting out the silhouette shape in a contact adhesive material and applying to the stone, or draw round a card cut-out. Outline the design with a felt-tipped pen or aluminium pencil.

Using a trim-saw, carefully cut away surplus stone as close to the template as possible. For difficult areas cut a series of close parallel saw-cuts towards the template or design mark (figure 121). It is essential to allow for the curvature of the saw-blade to prevent undercutting and a small angled support, which fits on the saw-

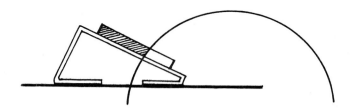

Figure 122. Angled support to present rock to saw blade at correct angle to prevent undercutting

bed, can be made to prevent this (figure 122). Break the thin stone projections left by the saw cuts. Further edge trimming and shaping can be done on silicon carbide grinding wheels and use can be made of a worn wheel, dressed to a bevelled rim for grinding into reticulated areas (figure 123). Continue trimming in this way until the design outline has been formed. Peel off the ad-

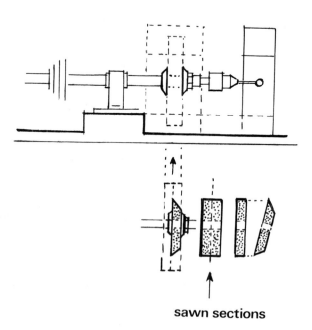

sawn sections

Figure 123. Worn down grinding wheels trimmed to shape on diamond saw and used on grinding shaft for carving

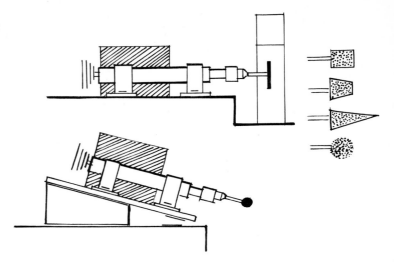

Figure 124. Horizontal and angled point carving machines, used with assorted abrasive points

hesive template and remove any trace of gum with methylated spirit. If the stone is too small to hold comfortably in the hand it should be dopped on a piece of wood.

The cut out blank is now ready for carving into a shallow relief by manipulating the stone against a range of tools selected for particular shapes and contours, which can be fitted into the chuck of a small point carving lathe (figure 124). Abrasive points of silicon carbide or aluminium oxide moulded in a wide selection of shapes can be employed. With these materials cutting techniques are simplified by having both hands available to hold the stone which is moved against the points during shaping. Water coolant should be applied frequently and care taken not to overheat the stone. Diamond impregnated carving tools may also be fitted to lathes or drills and working techniques are similar but it should be remembered that diamond cuts more rapidly.

Methods using silicon carbide loose grits of different grades are effective and economical but require a certain measure of dexterity. Small tools made of steel are improvized by the cutter to suit the work. The stone is held against the revolving tool with one hand and abrasive grit and water is applied to the work by a small brush in the other hand. To prevent grits being flung from the work, turning speeds of the shaft must be controlled by a multiple pulley system. Piercing and hollowing with loose grits can be achieved with ball points or sections of hollow tubing well supplied with abrasive slurry.

When the relief has been formed to satisfaction, the work can be refined by hand using fine silicon carbide sticks or wet/dry papers glued to shaped wooden points. Polishing is done with an assortment of cloth and felt buffing wheels charged with a slurry of an oxide suited to the particular stone. A polishing mop can be fitted into the carving lathe chuck and stone held against it.

Cameos

Cameos can be described as diminutive relief carvings with the pictorial image raised above the surface of a contrasting background. Light and dark layers of materials, such as the chalcedony varieties onyx and sardonyx, are suited to this form of decoration where a darker background gives emphasis to forms cut from the lighter layer. Shell cameos rely not so much on a severe dark and light contrast but on delicate colouration, translucency and a gradual tonal range, depending to a large extent on a subtle play of light and shade on the engraved forms. In many instances the backgrounds of shell cameos are artificially tinted to deepen colour and tone.

Many of the larger shells with a coloured layer structure, such as conch or king helmet, can be used and the lighter layers for the raised carving may be located either on external or internal portions. The helmet shell provides excellent cameo material with good contrast through layers of white to pale orange and brown. The translucency of the white layer can be used to advantage when sanded to a fine veneer, revealing undertones of glowing colour.

The softness of shell and the ease with which it can be sawn, scratched or carved makes this an ideal medium for the amateur cameo-cutter. Carving can be done by hand and a minimum of equipment is needed, most of the small tools being made from broken hacksaw blades as required. The extent of curvature and natural distortion of a shell often restricts the size of workable areas, particularly if the cameo is to be mounted on a ring or brooch setting where a flat base is needed.

Traditionally, portrait heads and figures are associated with cameos but natural forms are equally acceptable and the cutter should be guided by individual interests. Subject sources are numerous; either personal studies from direct observation or utilization of photographs and illustrations, preferable in black and white, with good tonal variation. A design may have to be drawn to reduced scale from the original photograph and then carefully traced ready for transfer to the piece of stone or shell.

CUTTING A SHELL CAMEO

Select a suitable portion of the shell showing two-tone layers in section and of a thickness to allow a shallow relief in the lighter part. Using a small diamond trim-saw or hacksaw, saw the shell to size. Mark out the perimeter shape (oval, square, rectangle) and cut with a fine hacksaw or a jewellers' piercing saw using careful downward cutting strokes. Clean up the edge with a smooth file or abrasive stick. Avoid harsh treatment as the material is brittle and in older shells the tendency to flake or crumble will be more pronounced.

The white or upper portion of the shell will receive the design and the coloured side will form the base of the cameo. Where thickness and minimum curvature will allow, a more level surface can sometimes be ground on the base. Rub the top or white surface lightly with a fine abrasive paper to remove any natural glossy coating and to facilitate transfer of the design.

To make handling easier during carving, the shell is mounted on a small block of wood slightly wider than the cameo blank. Warm a small quantity of jewellers' pitch in a container and warm the shell on a hot-plate but do not over-heat. Smear the heated pitch on the wooden block and press the shell on the tacky surface. Do not embed the shell too deeply; it must remain on the surface to enable the cutter to observe the thickness and to gauge the depth of cut. Allow to cool and harden thoroughly before continuing. Dopping wax will serve as a substitute adhesive but is rather brittle and needs a little beeswax adding to the molten mixture to improve its condition (figure 125).

To transfer the design, rub soft graphite pencil over the back of the drawing or use a piece of carbon paper under the tracing. Trace the outline of the design, using medium pressure with a hard grade of pencil, transferring an exact impression to the shell. If the design fails to register directly on the shell surface, paint on a

Figure 125. Carving cameo shell blank dopped on wooden block. Graver controlled by thumb pressure

layer of white poster colour (water soluble) and when dry retrace the design as before. With a fine pointed tool or graver score out the principal lines on the shell, including the basic silhouette shape, to fix the position of the design. Wash away all traces of the white paint if used.

The background areas of the design must now be lowered to isolate the raised portion of shell which forms the basis for the relief carving. Select a small chisel-shaped tool, such as a square graver, and carve a shallow groove around the design perimeter, working outside the line. Cut the remaining background areas up to the first groove, cutting inwards from the outer edge of the blank. This is important, as cutting towards the edge can result in crumbling of the shell as the tool rides across the rim. To prevent splitting or flaking when cutting larger background areas, do not hold the tool at a steep angle and avoid digging hard into the surface. Hold the tool almost parallel to the surface and use a series of short pushing or forward scraping actions. Control will develop with practice. For lowering isolated areas within the form, a rocking or walking action with the tip of the graver can be used. Gradually level the background to a depth of half the shell's thickness or until a satisfactory contrasting layer has been revealed.

Carving the raised portion requires care and patience and it must be remembered that the relief will be very shallow. Cut away further levels or depths before commencing on details. A feeling of three-dimensional form can only be suggested by subtle changes of light and shade over gentle curves, highlighted points or ridges, and sharply defined engraved lines. Edges of the forms should be carefully carved down to the background.

The selection of tools for each process will depend on the surface areas or desired finish treatment of the design; for example, sharp points for definition, chisel edges for broad smooth surfaces. A range of textures can be achieved by scoring with small toothed sections of a hacksaw blade or a multiple line graver.

Refinements can be made by rubbing with shaped silicon carbide sticks or with fine grades of wet/dry papers cut into small pieces to suit the purpose, for instance, folded into sharp ridges to sand vee-shaped cuts or wrapped around tapered sticks to make abrasive points. Fragments of moistened cloth dipped into fine grades of silicon carbide grit or powdered pumice can be used in a similar way for delicate smoothing.

A slurry of tin or cerium oxide applied with a cloth or chamois leather will add a final lustre, followed by a rub on a soft cloth to bring up the highlights on the raised forms. Wash away all traces of polishing oxide and remove cameo from pitch block by heating carefully (not directly exposed to flame) or by freezing for a short time. Any leverage under the cameo at the removal stage must be

Figure 126. Examples of shell cameos cut by a self-taught amateur, Mr. E. Rowberry, Hull, England

done gently to prevent cracking or crumbling of the edge (figure 126).

Carved shell cut-outs, including all types of shell reliefs and engravings in more colourful materials such as mother-of-pearl, abalone and paua shells, can follow the same mounting and cutting procedure. After removal from the pitch block the background is then sawn away with a piercing saw to outline the basic carved form.

Intaglio and engraving

Designs carved or engraved below the surface of a gem mineral are cut *intaglio* and form a complete contrast to cameos and carving in relief (figure 127). Cutting an intaglio calls for considerable skill and appreciation of forms in reverse order, presenting a negative image with the material being totally removed from the design. Originally cut as seals or ring-stones, this type of inverted carving reproduces an exact raised impression in softened wax. Although the demand for gem intaglios for use as seals has diminished, hand-cut stones are still produced by lapidary craftsmen for setting in rings.

Before attempting intaglio carving the beginner would be

Figure 127. (Top) Intaglio cut from smoky quartz. (Bottom) cameo cut from brown chalcedony. (Geological Museum, London.) Crown copyright, Geological Survey photograph. Reproduced by permission of the Controller, HMSO

advised to complete several cameos or small relief carvings in shell and stone of different hardnesses to get the feeling for tools and cutting characteristics of the materials. Select a finished relief carving and press into a bed of plasticine, modelling clay or tray of softened wax; carefully withdrawing it to leave a clear impression. This is an excellent way to appreciate the inverted form and the changing levels of details.

CUTTING A DEEP INTAGLIO

Choose a suitable subject such as a portrait head, bird or animal and decide on appropriate materials and tools. Fine, precise details will be more durable in a harder mineral of compact and uniform composition. Brittle stones or those with pronounced cleavage should not be used. Intaglios can be cut into any pre-shaped surface whether domed, cylindrical, concave or flat but working into a flat face presents fewer complications.

Trim a slab on a diamond saw, flat on both sides as for a cabochon blank, and lap both surfaces until level. The perimeter shape is a matter of choice and can be formed on a grinding wheel. Dop the stone on a small block of wood for easy handling and transfer the design to the upper surface. This can be done by cutting a silhouette template from stiff paper or thin card and drawing round the edge with an aluminium pencil or felt-tipped marker.

Using ball-tipped abrasive tools fitted to drills or a point carving lathe, the first step will be to hollow out a depression equal in volume to the basic mass of the three-dimensional subject. Forget about details until later stages. Take a wax impression from the hollowed-out area and assess the position and shape of further raised portions required to build up a wax facsimile of the finished work. Drill out these additional forms from the stone, remembering that work will be in reverse and forms which occur on the left side of the wax impression will be on the right when cutting into the stone. Further wax impressions should be taken at each stage as the drill probes deeper into the inverted forms. Smaller cutting tools will be used as work progresses. When the main forms and contours have been established, subtle variations and refinements of the broad shapes can be introduced and the upper edge more sharply defined. Finally add the required details of the subject with finest cutting points.

When cutting is completed, accessible areas within the cavity can be smoothed with abrasive pastes or slurries by using tapered felts and mops fitted into a drill chuck. Polish the flat outer surface surrounding the intaglio, but not the engraved portion, to form a better contrast. Quite often the final result will create an optical illusion of relief carving when viewed in certain lights.

Cutting techniques and the choice of tools will vary with

individuals but it may be found convenient to have the carving points in a fixed position either vertically or near horizontal (tilted downwards at a slight angle) and the hand-held stone manipulated against the revolving points. Dipping the work in a container of water will wash away slurry and provide coolant and lubricant during cutting.

ENGRAVED OR SHALLOW INTAGLIOS

On softer cutting materials surface incisions can be made with a variety of tools such as hand engravers, points and gouges made from broken hacksaw-blades and sharpened nails. Silicon carbide sticks and pieces of broken grinding wheels can be sawn to various shapes for scoring surfaces. Power operated points, burrs and a wide range of small discs can be fixed in small hand tools or flexible drive drill attachments.

The material to be engraved can be dopped on a block of wood and held firmly on the bench with one hand or secured in a small vice. Sometimes it is necessary to have the work free to rotate for cutting in different directions or turning against the graver to assist in formulating continuous curves. To aid this process the block can be supported on a small leather bag of sand with a curved base for easy turning on the bench. The work and support turn simultaneously. Hand engraving tools are made with small handles which fit comfortably in the palm of the hand as the tool is pushed forward or rocked against the work (figure 128).

Engraved designs can be entirely linear, cut at varying depths and thicknesses, or contrasted with textured backgrounds of opposing lines and cross hatching. Portions not engraved can be highly polished to provide changing surface qualities (figure 129).

Figure 128. (Below) Engraving tool held in correct position

Figure 129. (Below right) Examples of floral decoration and monogram engraved on Whitby jet

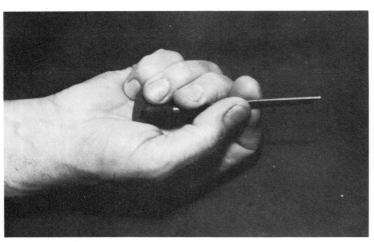

Bowls and vases

Stone selected for shaping into bowls and vases should be tough, compact material without flaws or fractures. Brittle varieties which easily chip or flake and those with pronounced planes of cleavage are unsuitable. Generally, the workable proportions of fracture-free material are limited and avoidance of any imperfections will often determine the size and shape of the object to be worked. Allowing for pre-forming and shaping, the original piece of stone will be considerably reduced in weight and scale on completion of the project.

Bowls and vases are shaped by a process of turning or gradual abrasion of a stone which is securely dopped to a rotating face-plate or mounting head on either a horizontal or vertical shaft (figure 130). Abrasive cutting tools are hand-held against the workpiece, shaping internal and external surfaces while the revolving form remains perfectly symmetrical around its central axis. The face-plate to which the stone is attached can be screwed to the arbor of the driving shaft or held in the securing chuck of a lathe. Small powered bench lathes used for wood and metal turning are suitable or standard lapidary machines with simple modifications can be utilized. Many cutters improvize shafts, arbor attachments and mounting heads at little cost.

Face-plates or mounting heads for the stones can be of any suitable diameter depending on the scale of work being attempted. However, it is important to avoid metal projections beyond the base diameters of the bowl or vase where there is any likelihood of interference with cutting and manipulation of tools. Mounting a

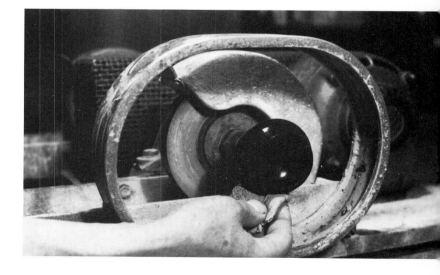

Figure 130. Polishing a small serpentine bowl. Dopped to a metal face-plate and turned on a horizontal shaft. The small diameter face-plate replaced the sanding disc attachment on a standard lapidary machine

stone too large for the size of the shaft is not only dangerous but may upset the entire balance of the shaft and distort the symmetry of the work being formed. The beginner is advised to concentrate on miniature creations with subtle profile shapes.

Machines used for turning should be equipped with a speed change system, allowing for low speeds between 700 and 850 rev/min for preliminary shaping, increasing as work progresses within limitations of control and safety. A water coolant system must be employed which directs fluid to the cutting area through a fine pipe or hose, with splash guards and a slurry collecting trough under the work. Excessive coolant flow will create too much spray and obscure the work progress. Protective goggles are recommended to guard against grit impregnated spray and small stone chips. It is prudent to stand or sit slightly to one side of the work during cutting and so be outside the centrifugal path of any ejected debris.

Silicon carbide sticks of different grades make excellent shaping tools and are quite adequate for stones in the lower hardness group (figure 131). Shaping is considerably slower on agates and stones of similar hardness but small abrasive wheels used on a flexible drive, held to revolve in counter direction to the stone, will produce evenly hollowed surfaces most effectively. Soft stones respond to an assortment of steel turning tools, rasps and files, which must be cleaned and dried after use to prevent rusting.

Figure 131. Shaping sticks made from worn silicon carbide grinding wheels

Rust stains can be difficult to remove if allowed to impregnate porous stones.

For surface smoothing, rubber-bonded silicon carbide or aluminium oxide sticks and small diameter wheels can be employed by hand or in a flexible drive shaft. Alternatively, wet/dry sanding cloth or paper can be held against the work with the fingers or may be wrapped around conveniently shaped sticks. Water coolant should still be applied during sanding. For polishing, small pieces of hard felt or leather impregnated with a slurry of polishing oxide can be applied to the work but overheating must not occur.

SECURING THE STONE

Dopping or cementing the stone to the face-plate or mounting head can be done by using cold epoxy cements liberally supplied to both support and stone then firmly pressed together. Centre the stone and hold in a fixed position until set to prevent sliding. Additional applications of cement are made as required. Alternatively the stone can be mounted by using a heated dopping wax of standard content consisting basically of plaster of paris, sealing wax and shellac. If the wax appears too brittle in use it may be reconditioned by adding a little beeswax to the mixture. A ready made dopping wax is obtainable in blocks or sticks from most lapidary suppliers. In some areas of Britain, craftsmen in small village industries turning objects from ornamental serpentine use dopping cement made of plaster of paris, beeswax and pine resins which effectively secures the stones.

Using the molten wax method of dopping, the mounting head and base of stone must be heated prior to applying the hot wax. While the wax is still soft try to centre the stone as near as possible by visual means and then add further wax to build up a good support. Wait until the wax or cement is thoroughly hardened before starting to turn the object.

To remove a completed vase or bowl, the dopping wax can be carefully reheated and any wax on the base of the work can be cleaned off with methylated spirits. With epoxy cements the turned object will have to be removed by careful sawing with a hacksaw, cutting through the cement at the base of the stone. This can best be accomplished while the face-plate is still attached to the lathe, or it can be removed and the stone separated by using a diamond saw. During these operations the bowl or vase must be wrapped to protect the surfaces and well cushioned to prevent breakage. An appropriate resin solvent should be obtained to clean off surplus cement.

The task will be made easier if as much waste material as possible is removed from the stone prior to mounting on the lathe and carefully planned use of a diamond saw will assist shaping. The turned form will be symmetical and circular in cross section at any point with uniform projections and hollows around the circumference, therefore the basic starting shape should be cylindrical. In order to achieve this, first slab the rough into square section, feeding to the saw blade by hand if the stone is too big to fit the vice. Draw circles on the end faces and make a series of cuts parallel to the central axis, removing the corners along the total length. Further trimming and refinements to remove excess material may be possible. Hollowing out bowl interiors can be assisted by pre-forming with a small diameter saw blade; make a number of cuts close together across the diameter then carefully break out the pieces of stone which are left (figure 132).

The pre-form can now be dopped on the face-plate but it is essential to centre the stone to ensure even revolutions. If it is too much off-centre considerable bumping will occur and the resultant vibrations may unseat the stone. Some cutters overcome this problem by cementing the rough piece of stone (flat at both ends) to the face-plate before any sawing or shaping takes place. When the cement is set the machine is switched on and a scriber or marker held against the end section near to the edge of the

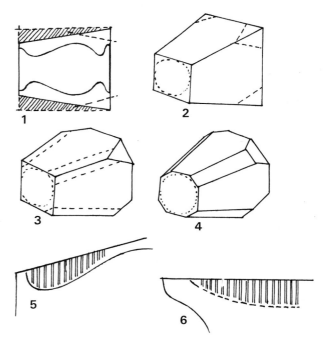

Figure 132. Use of slab/trim saw to aid pre-forming small vases and bowls, prior to mounting on lathe: (1–4) progressive stages in removing unwanted parts of block to give basic starting shape for turning; (5) further shaping possible by making close parallel saw-cuts and breaking off pieces remaining; (6) hollowing out a bowl or vase top can be started by making saw-cuts with small diameter blade for shallow curvatures

148

stone. A perfectly centred circle is inscribed on the stone and then a series of straight lines can be drawn outside the circle to indicate the position of saw cuts. This method is possible when the face-plate attachment is small enough to remove from the shaft with the stone in position and does not interfere with the sawing.

With the stone firmly cemented in position continue pre-forming with the machine running at a slow speed, between 700 and 850 rev/min, to remove ridges left by sawing and so balance the stone correctly. If using a lathe toolrest make sure this is clear of any projecting points of stone. Select a coarse grit silicon carbide stick and hold at a steep upward angle against the stone, allowing projections to drag against the abrasive surface. The stone is rotating towards the cutter while the abrasive tool is relatively static. Do not push the stick horizontally or downwards into the stone at this stage to avoid any possibility of it becoming wedged between stone and workrest. Use moderate pressure and keep firm control of the abrasive tool to counteract vibration and bumping which is inevitable until the stone is properly centred. As the rough portions of stone are gradually removed along the full length the abrasion will become smoother, allowing a freer movement of the tool from side to side until the pre-form is running in perfect balance round its axis. Remember to have adequate coolant supply on the work.

SHAPING AND POLISHING

Increase the turning speed to about 1500 rev/min or approximate speed convenient for stepped pulley combinations in use, and continue cutting with the 100 grit abrasive tool. The true shaping of either bowl or vase can now begin, either working to a pre-conceived design or carving intuitively as work progresses, developing hollowed and raised forms and elegance of outline.

The abrasive cutting tool held in one position against the stone will gradually form a depression conforming to the shape of the tool. By applying pressure from left to right the groove can be widened and shaped to a smooth convex form. It is important to hold the tool at 90 degrees to the stone as any deviation will produce irregularity in the profile shape.

When a satisfactory shape has been achieved change to finer abrasive tools, 220 grit in the case of silicon carbide, or equivalent aluminium oxide wheels or sticks. Remove marks and scratches from the previous coarse shaping stage and refine the whole surface area of the work. Water coolant must be used throughout the entire grinding and sanding operations.

Hollowing out the opening in a vase or bowl is performed in a similar manner and the work rest and coolant hose should be moved to new positions. Various stages of abrasion are carried out

Figure 133. Turned serpentine bowl

Figure 134. Bowl turned from translucent onyx (calcite)

until a satisfactory opening has been formed and the walls are of the required thickness.

Sanding can be done with various grades of wet/dry paper or cloth held in the fingers against the contours of the stone as it turns. Specially shaped sanding sticks can be made by gluing abrasive papers onto pieces of wood. Periodically, stop the machine and inspect the work carefully, turning it slowly by hand. Make sure all grinding marks are removed and the surface is perfectly smooth.

The final polishing is carried out at the slowest speed, taking care not to overheat the stone as the thin walls are easily shattered at this stage. Using pads of felt or leather and a slurry of cerium or tin oxide continue the polishing process until a satisfactory finish is obtained (figures 133, 134).

When turning stones of tough composition or in the higher hardness range the use of diamond abrasives will speed up the cutting processes. Cutting can be done with an assortment of rigid tools, wheels and discs impregnated with finely bonded diamond grits, but the use of pastes and compounds for refining the shaped contours would be uneconomical owing to wastage and loss of grit particles spun off the turning surface of the stone.

Considering that much of the popular material for turning and carving will be under hardness 7 (Mohs' scale), silicon carbide abrasives for shaping and sanding may be adequate for general use.

Cutting spheres and beads

Polished spheres and beads cut from a variety of minerals can be attractively displayed or drilled for use as jewellery. Whatever the purpose, fashioning stone spheres can be as absorbing as other lapidary activities and attracts a growing number of enthusiasts.

As sphere-making equipment uses silicon carbide grits for much of the shaping and finishing, a full range of gem material can be processed, from agate to onyx marble, by choosing suitable abrasive combinations. Stones selected for cutting ornamental spheres should possess qualities of visual interest such as colour and variation in pattern or banding. Brittle stones and those with pronounced cleavage should not be used. Careful examination should be made for fractures and other structural flaws but hard and soft portions, inclusions or minute cavities below the surface are not always apparent until cutting commences. Many stones are known to have these characteristics and can be avoided altogether or cut in the hope of grinding beyond the trouble spots, thus reducing the size of the sphere. If these problems persist, however, the stone should be abandoned.

PRE-FORMING

By using progressive stages of sawing and grinding the stone is cut into rough spherical shape before sanding on a sphere-making machine. Start in a modest way and plan the size of the sphere to suit available equipment, for example standard machines with six to eight-inch grinding wheels will enable spheres up to two inches in diameter to be ground against the wheel to remove points and projections following pre-shaping with a slabbing saw. When grinding avoid bumping and 'chattering' of the stone against the wheel which should have a level face and not be grooved. The use of a work rest in front of the wheel will provide greater stability and facilitate handling.

Select the stone and slab into a cube, then draw a circle on one face to suggest the approximate diameter of the finished sphere.

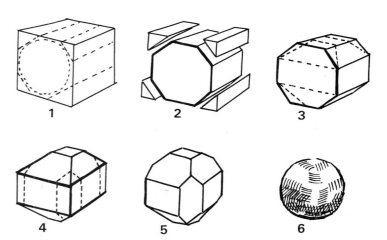

Figure 135. Sequences in pre-forming a sphere by sawing and then grinding down the points and ridges in readiness for the sphere-making machine

By making a series of saw cuts, as shown in the diagrams (figure 135) a round shape will begin to emerge. Carefully grind off the points and round off flat faces to achieve the desired shape. A circular template cut in a sheet of card can be used for testing the shape. When the preform is satisfactorily rounded it can be transferred to sphere cutting equipment for further refinements and polishing.

Stone off-cuts sawn from preforms may be suitable for cabochons, tumbling or mosaics and should be placed in a box kept near to the saw for retaining usable pieces.

SPHERE MACHINES

Automatic sphere cutters consist of two angled shafts rotating in opposing directions. A number of variously-sized cups, with inward bevelled rims which assist abrasive and polishing actions, are attached to facing ends of the shafts and support the stone during cutting (figure 136). The cup should be about two-thirds of the stone's diameter. The stone is held in position by controlled pressure enabling free rotation in all directions and can be adjusted by horizontal movement. Two separate motor and pulley drives are involved, geared to the required speed reduction of about 150 to 200 rev/min for larger spheres and 300 to 400 rev/min for smaller ones.

To operate, a rounded preform is correctly adjusted between the cups and rotation commenced. Start with coarse abrasion for removal of all points and bumps and proceed through medium and fine stages until satisfied the sphere is perfectly smooth and free from blemishes of any kind. Slurries of grit and water are brushed on the revolving stone as required. Before going on to the polishing stage all traces of grit must be washed away from the machine, stone and hands.

Secure a pad of leather, felt or closely woven canvas over the ends of the cups and brush on a polishing oxide mixture. Replace the sphere in position and add an occasional squirt of water or further applications of polish as needed.

ALTERNATIVE METHOD

Sanding of spheres can be done on vertical shaft attachments, directly involving the cutter in the shaping process. A short metal tube can either be screwed directly on the shaft or dopped on a metal lap plate, geared to turn at the slowest speed for maximum control. A second tube held in the hand steadies the preform and ensures even distribution of abrasive grits (figure 137). As the sphere rotates it is manipulated in all directions by light pressures on the hand-held tube. Too much pressure may result in a circular

Figure 136. Motorized sphere-making machine: (Above) sanding phases with loose grits; (Below) finishing process using polishing oxides on covered sphere cups.

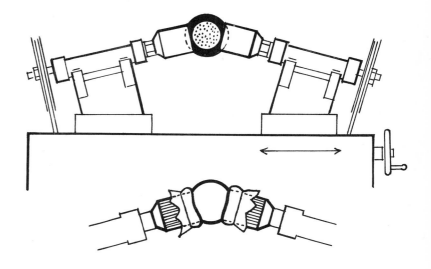

Figure 137. Sanding and polishing spheres by hand, using metal cup dopped to a lap and section of metal tube

groove being cut into the surface of the preform. Abrasive slurries are applied to the sphere as previously outlined. In some cases the second tube is dispensed with and pads of leather used with grits, or wet/dry abrasive cloths, are held directly on the sphere by hand.

To polish, a piece of canvas, leather or felt is tied securely to the lower tube and coated with creamy polishing medium. A further piece of material is held in contact with the sphere as it rotates.

Figure 138. Spheres made by hand methods

Figure 139. Gemstone egg shaped and polished by hand

If preferred, polishing buffs can be attached to the second tube and rocked over the sphere in the same manner as before (figure 138).

BEAD MAKING

Beads and small spheres can be turned in machines of similar design, using two rotating cups, but constructed on a smaller scale. A third cup or forming stick can be fixed or hand held against the spheres to speed up shaping during grit stages. At the polishing stage, small spheres can be dopped in conical ended dop sticks and polished in the same way as cabochons on a buffing wheel. Polish

Figure 140. A beadmill, worked from a drill press, with attachments for processing beads and small spheres of different sizes

one half of the sphere and then re-dop to complete the other side.

Bead mills can be obtained which, simultaneously, will shape a number of beads to uniform size. As in tumbling, stones of similar hardness must be processed at the same time to prevent uneven wear. The bead mill illustrated (figure 140) works from a drill press with the turning plate secured in the drill chuck, but other bead mills operate as self-contained units powered by $\frac{1}{4}$ hp motors. The bed of the mill has a continuous groove cut to take the bead preforms which revolve in slurries of abrasive grits, progressing from coarse to fine. Polishing attachments can be fitted to some bead mills for final processing but all grits must be cleaned from the grinding bowl before use. Hand finishing methods are also employed as outlined previously, by dopping the small rounded stones and polishing on buffing wheels. It is possible to drill quantities of beads following abrasive stages and tumble polish a batch in small capacity barrels. Use cerium oxide or tin oxide, together with plastic granules or other additives to prevent fracturing around the edges of the drilled holes.

Inlay, mosaic and intarsia

Basic materials for these decorative crafts are easy to obtain and use can be made of pebbles or tumble polished stones, broken rock fragments and trimsaw offcuts to hand in most lapidary workshops. Equipment for sawing, lapping and shaping stones

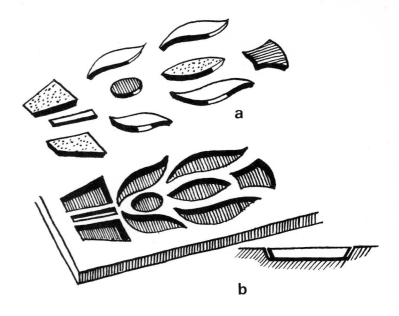

is necessary for the more exacting applications of inlay and intarsia. The type of backing support used and choice of adhesives and cements will depend on selected projects. Designs should be carefully worked out on paper beforehand.

INLAY

The design shapes are cut away to form shallow depressions in the background material and replaced or inlaid with different stones cut to precise dimensions (figure 141). A soft background stone should be chosen to simplify drilling and formation of the design cavities and should also provide a contrast of tone and colour to the inlay. Areas of darkly toned marbles and slates are often used as neutral grounds for brightly coloured and patterned insets of stone and shell.

Surface backgrounds should be level or smoothly contoured and sanded to a matt finish for transfer of the design. Outline the shapes to be removed with fine abrasive points and lower the internal portions using appropriate drills and burrs. Level off the base of the cavities and ensure the sides are sharply cut and tapered to uniform depth.

Take a sheet of thin paper and place it on the prepared background surface, securing it with cellulose tape if needed to prevent slipping. Using a wax crayon or soft pencil, rub over the paper in different directions until the outline of the hollowed patterns becomes clearly defined. Remove the paper and insert an identifying number in each of the rubbed pattern shapes to correspond with coded diagram previously worked out of the various coloured stones which are to form the inlays.

To prepare the inlays, choose suitable pieces of stone, trim to thin slices on a diamond saw and reduce further on the lap. Cut out the rubbed shapes from the paper pattern and gum them to the selected stones to serve as templates. Use a trimsaw to isolate different shapes from the stones. Grind to the edges of the patterns by careful cutting on six-inch or four-inch grinding wheels. Where control is difficult smaller abrasive wheels attached to carving heads can be used. A flexible drive chuck held in a clamp can operate small diameter wheels, leaving both hands free to manipulate pieces of stone with intricate outlines.

When the shapes are cut the paper is removed from one piece at a time and the stone fixed in the correct cavity with a quick-drying, waterproof adhesive such as epoxy resin. If the adhesive is tinted to match the background colour it can be forced into any gaps and levelled off to conceal sections which are not a perfect fit. When the inlaid design is completely set the entire surface can be sanded over before polishing by hand or rotary buffing wheel.

MOSAIC

Small pieces of stone, cemented into position on a firm backing, can be used to build up a picture or design. The pieces may be uniform in size and shape, for example squares and rectangles, or irregular in outline and dimensions. Interpretations of the subjects must be suited to the medium of mosaic and natural forms simplified to flat areas of graduated colours, accented where required with definite boundary outlines (figure 142). The

Figure 142. Alternative mosaic treatment: (a) Accentuated boundary outlines to design shapes; (b) boundary edges formed through contrasts of colour and tone

a   b

angular shape of mosaic squares is suited to geometric abstract designs. Possible projects include wall panels and plaques, coffee tables, trays, lampbases and garden ornaments.

Materials frequently used include all types of marble, ceramic tiles and specially made forms of glass, but for the lapidary natural stones may be preferred. Gemstone slabs, polished or unpolished, can be broken into small pieces or trimmed on a diamond saw into squares and rectangles. Colour schemes will be determined by the range of gem rough available. Marble chippings and pebbles can be used as background fillers.

The backing supports can be of plywood, chipboard or compressed hardboard with rough and smooth faces. These materials are absorbent and should be given one or two coatings of shellac on both sides. Glass fibre and resins may also be used in the creation of mosaics. Various forms of adhesive, such as a P.V.A. glue or an epoxy resin, are used to fix the pieces of stone in position. Tile cements or special mosaic cements are obtainable from craft suppliers under various trade names. A waterproof grouting is preferable for levelling spaces between the stones when the work is completed and colouring agents or stains can be added to the grouting if desired.

Mosaic pieces can be applied to backing supports by either the direct or indirect methods. Of the two, the direct method is less involved but will require stone pieces slabbed to the same thickness if a level surface is required. With polished gemstones irregularity of heights and angles may be advantageous to reflect light and add a textural variation. The direct method is also suited to curved and angular surfaces and is used to apply mosaic decoration to walls.

Direct method

Select the backing, cut to required proportions and seal all porous surfaces with shellac. Trace the design directly on the backing and strengthen the outlines with a fine brush and waterproof ink. To apply the mosaic, spread adhesive over a limited portion of the design and press stones into position right side uppermost (figure 143). Apply only as much adhesive as can be covered by mosaic within the setting time. Areas can be covered progressively across the design commencing at one edge or corner, alternatively all the main outlines can be completed first, filling in the enclosures at later stages.

When the design is complete, spaces between the stones are filled with grouting cement and sponged level. Surplus cement is then removed and the whole is allowed to set thoroughly. Applications of wax polish and a rub with a soft cloth will greatly improve the surface appearance of the mosaic.

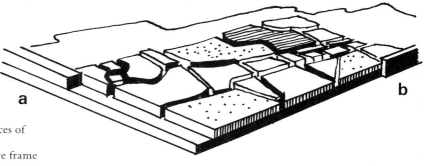

Figure 143. Direct method: pieces of same thickness applied right side uppermost; (a) and (b) alternative frame or edging positions

Indirect method

An advantage with this method is that all the flat faces of the stones will be level even though the pieces are of different thicknesses and the undersides roughly shaped as these will be concealed in the cement (figure 144). As the mosaic surface will be laid upside down in this case, trace the design in reverse (left becomes right) on a sheet of paper. Select pieces of stone, lapped and polished on one side only, and paste them into position face downwards on the paper. Water soluble paste must be used. Complete the whole design in this way, making full use of random shaped offcuts as well as pieces specially trimmed for the purpose.

There are several methods of backing the stones when using the indirect method, but the following procedure is simple and effective for producing framed mosaic panels. Place a retaining frame around the stones, measured and cut to enclose the design. Spread the mosaic cement inside the frame until it is level with the

Figure 144. Indirect method: sliced pebbles and slabs of different thicknesses applied in reverse

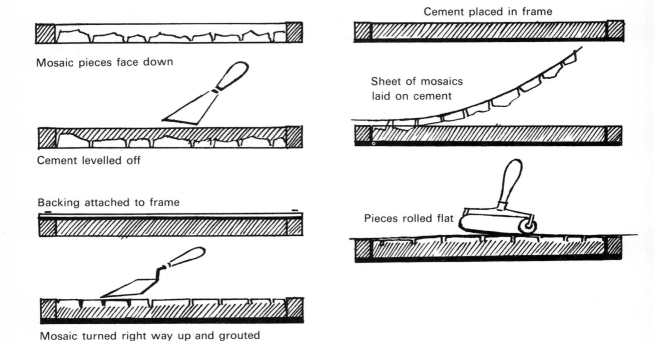

Mosaic pieces face down

Cement placed in frame

Cement levelled off

Sheet of mosaics
laid on cement

Backing attached to frame

Pieces rolled flat

Mosaic turned right way up and grouted

Figure 145. Indirect method: two ways of cementing mosaic pieces; (a) frame built round mosaic, infilled with cement to cover pieces; (b) cement placed in completed form for embedding sheet of mosaic

top and covering the highest point of the stones (figure 145). Allow reasonable time for the cement to set. Cut a backing board to the size of the frame and stick it down on the mosaic cement. Finally, screw or tack the board to the back of the frame. Turn the panel over and remove the paper from the mosaic by soaking with water and scraping gently. Use grouting cement as before to fill in spaces. Clean and wax polish the surface.

Alternative methods can be used to attach the completed sheet of mosaic pieces to the cement backing, for example the cement can be prepared within a panel of given size and the entire sheet lifted up and placed carefully on the cement bed with the paper side uppermost. A roller is then applied to the surface to level off the mosaic pieces and embed them securely in the cement. Lifting the mosaic sheet is more easily accomplished with the assistance of another person to place it in position accurately. As before, when the cement is set, the paper is removed from the mosaic surface and grouting applied.

Polyester resin with glass fibre reinforcement provides an excellent adhesive and rigid backing for stone mosaics, using both direct and indirect methods, and is favoured by many for making small table tops.

The arrangement of pieces is similar to the assembly of a closely interlocking jigsaw and the stones are slabbed and trimmed to precise patterns, each piece fitting exactly to the contours of adjacent shapes. Designs must be simple to execute and pictorial themes, if attempted, must be decorative and uncomplicated. Stones can either be selected to interpret colours and textures of the original design or a composition can be planned to use available gemstone material. The direct method of applying intarsia pieces is considered most suitable as comparisons can be made at any time with the prepared design. The slabs used should be of uniform thickness and sanded smooth on both sides. Polishing can be done either before or after completing the design but in some cases the appearance is improved by leaving a matt finish.

To make a flat intarsia panel, carefully trace the whole design on paper to the exact size of the original. Sharpen up the main outlines of the design with a pen or fine brush. Using careful judgment, divide up the main shapes into smaller units of suitable proportions for the gem rough selected (figure 146). Place an

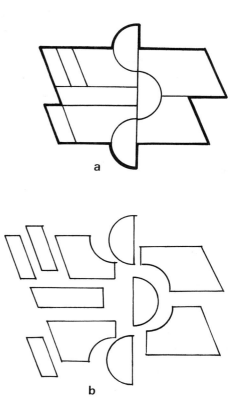

Figure 146. (a) Intarsia design; (b) pattern shapes isolated as templates for individual stone pieces

Figure 147. A fine example of intarsia inlaid into black marble plateau. (Geological Museum, London). Materials used include other marbles, barytes, fluorite, malachite and mother-of-pearl. Crown copyright Geological Survey photograph, reproduced by permission of the Controller, HMSO

identifying mark on the design shapes and appropriate slabs. When every shape has been accounted for cut them from the paper and stick down on the slabs with water soluble paste or peel-off gum. The paper patterns now form templates to guide the sawing and shaping operations. As the stone shapes are prepared they can be assembled on the backing for trial fitting, and finally glued into position.

Appendix

Table 1 Main angles considered to be suitable guides for planning a series of facet cuts

Gem Mineral	Crown main	Pavilion main	Hardness (Mohs)	Refractive index	Critical angle
Andalusite	43	39	$7\frac{1}{2}$	1·62–1·64	38
Apatite	43	39	5	1·64	38
Beryl	42	43	$7\frac{1}{2}$–8	1·57–1·59	39
Chrysoberyl	37	42	$8\frac{1}{2}$	1·74–1·75	35
Corundum	37	42	9	1·76–1·77	35
Dioptase	40	40	5	1·64–1·70	37
Epidote	36	42	$6\frac{1}{2}$	1·72–1·78	35
Fluorite	41	45	4	1·43	44
Garnet	37	42	$6\frac{1}{2}$–$7\frac{1}{2}$	1·75–1·83	34–35
Kyanite	40	40	5–7	1·71–1·73	36
Peridot	43	39	$6\frac{1}{2}$–7	1·67	37
Prehnite	40	40	6–$6\frac{1}{2}$	1·61–1·64	38
Quartz	45/42	43	7	1·55	40
Spinel	37	42	8	1·72	36
Spodumene	43	39	$6\frac{1}{2}$–7	1·66–1·67	37
Topaz	43	39	8	1·61–1·63	38
Tourmaline	43	39	7–$7\frac{1}{2}$	1·62–1·64	38
Zircon	35	41	$7\frac{1}{2}$	1·93	31
Zircon	37	42	$6\frac{1}{2}$–7	1·82	34

Note: Rigid adherance to main angles is not absolutely vital and a few degrees variation is permissible in some stones to meet particular requirements providing pavilion angles do not fall below critical angles. The critical angles shown in the table, based on the refractive indices of the listed minerals, denote the limits for total internal reflection of the incident light rays. As the refractive index increases the critical angle is reduced. Pavilion angles cut lower than the critical angle will cause the light rays to pass out of the stone and a lifeless gem or one of considerably reduced brilliance will result.

To calculate other facet angles from the table:

Standard Brilliant

    Crown mains   Cut angles listed for particular gem material.

    Star facets   Subtract approximately 15 degrees from main angles.

    Girdle facets   From 2 degrees to 5 degrees higher than mains. The final angle will have to be reached in easy stages depending on proportions of the stone.

    Pavilion mains   Cut angles listed for gem material.

    Girdle facets   Commence approximately 2 degrees higher than mains angles – increase as necessary in easy stages.

Table 1 (*continued*)

Step cut stones.

   Individual decisions will have to be made regarding shape and number of facets required to suit the depth of the stone. Proportions to aim for are, crown – one third and pavilion – two thirds of total depth.

Crown step facets   Two or three in number; angles decreasing from the girdle up to the table.

Pavilion step facets   Three to five in number; angles decrease downwards to the culet or last facet, which is the listed main angle.

Calculate from the known factors ie the main angles listed in the tables for a particular mineral and plan the steps to change in five to ten degree stages. The changes in degrees need not necessarily be the same for both crown and pavilion steps providing the main angles remain fairly constant.

Table 2 Immersion fluids

Many of the immersion fluids which can be used in testing crystals for possible flaws are poisonous and are best avoided by those not familiar with the use of chemicals of this nature. Among the simpler fluids with less risks are

Fluids	R.I.
Water	1·33
Paraffin (kerosene)	1·45
Olive oil	1·47
Turpentine	1·47
Glycerine	1·47
Mineral oil	1·48
Oil of cedarwood	1·51
Oil of cloves	1·54
Oil of anise	1·55
Refractol	1·56
Oil of cinnamon	1·62

Most of the dangerous immersion fluids occur in a higher refractive index range but many of the fluids mentioned above will reveal the presence of pronounced flaws even in crystals of high R.I. when examined in a beam of light.

Table 3 Recommended mountings for grinding wheels and diamond saw blades.

Grinding wheel diameter (in.)	Diameter of Flanged collar (in.)	Shaft diameter (in.)
6	2	$\frac{5}{8}$
8	3	$\frac{3}{4}$
10	$3\frac{1}{2}$	1

Saw blade diameter (in.)	Diameter of Flat collar (in.)	Shaft diameter (in.)
6 to 10	2 to $2\frac{1}{2}$	$\frac{5}{8}$
10 to 14	$2\frac{1}{2}$ to $3\frac{1}{2}$	$\frac{3}{4}$
18 to 20	$4\frac{1}{2}$ to 5	1
24	6	$1\frac{1}{4}$

Maximum safe operating speeds for grinding wheels and diamond saws are usually stated by manufacturers and shaft rev/min reductions are necessary as diameters increase to retain safe peripheral speeds.

Table 4 Peripheral speeds in surface feet per minute for wheels and blades and required rev/min (revolutions per minute).

Diameter in inches	Peripheral or rim speed in feet per minute					
	1000	2000	3000	4000	5000	6000
	Required revolutions per minute					
4	955	1910	2865	3820	4776	5731
6	637	1273	1910	2546	3183	3819
8	478	955	1433	1910	2388	2865
10	382	764	1146	1528	1910	2292

Operating speeds suggested for different processes:

Sawing (slabbing and trimming)   Rim speeds from 2500 to 8000 surface feet per minute. Dense, hard material: 2500 to 4000 surface feet per minute. Softer material: 4000 surface feet per minute upwards

Grinding   Peripheral speeds from 4000 to 6000 surface feet per minute.
   Caution: Do not exceed maximum rev/min (revolutions per minute) stated on grinding wheel.

Sanding   Discs, drums, belts, from 2500 to 4000 surface feet per minute

Polishing   Felt – 500 to 1000 surface feet per minute. Leather – 1000 to 2000 surface feet per minute. Muslin – 2000 to 3000 surface feet per minute

Note: Standard lapidary machines provide suitable pulley ratios to give appropriate speeds within the stated ranges

Table 5 Tumbler speeds

Diameter of drum	Recommended speeds
6 in. (152 mm)	35 to 50 rev/min.
8 in. (203 mm)	30 to 45 rev/min.
10 in. (254 mm)	25 to 40 rev/min.
12 in. (305 mm)	20 to 30 rev/min.

The slower speeds are recommended for angular barrels and also round drums loaded with brittle or very soft stones

Further Reading

A Textbook of Mineralogy, W. E. Ford, John Wiley (New York 1932).

Collecting and Polishing Stones, Herbert Scarfe, B. T. Batsford (London 1970).

Comprehensive Faceting Instructions, D. L. Hoffman, Aurora Lapidary Books (USA 1968).

Cutting and Setting Stones, Herbert Scarfe, B. T. Batsford (London 1972).

Discovering Lapidary Work, J. Wainwright, Mills and Boon (London 1971).

Facet Cutters Handbook, E. J. Soukup, Gembooks (California 1962).

Faceting for Amateurs, G. and M. Vargas, Desert Printers (California 1969).

Gemcraft, Lelande Quick and Hugh Leiper, Pitman (London) and Chilton, (Philadelphia 1960).

Gem Cutting, J. Sinkankas, Van Nostrand Co (USA 1962).

Gemmologists Compendium, R. Webster, N.A.G. Press (London 1964).

Gems and Gem Materials, Edward H. Kraus and Chester B. Slawson, McGraw-Hill (New York 1947).

Gems and Gemmology, C. J. Parsons and E. J. Soukup, Gembooks (California 1961).

Gems—their sources, descriptions and identification, R. Webster, Butterworths (London) and Shoe String (Hamden, Connecticut 1962).

Gemstones, H. G. F. Smith, Revised edition, Chapman and Hall (London 1973).

Gemstones of North America, J. Sinkankas, Van Nostrand Co (USA 1972).

Gem Testing, B. W. Anderson, Heywood and Co. (London 1958).

Pebbles as a Hobby, Janet Barber, Pelham Books (London 1972).
Practical Gemmology, R. Webster, N.A.G. Press (London 1966).
Practical Gemstone Craft, Helen Hutton, Studio Vista (London 1972).
Standard Catalogue of Gems, J. Sinkankas, Van Nostrand Co. (USA 1968).
The Gem Kingdom, Paul E. Desautels, Macdonald (London 1971).
Minerals and Man, Cornelius S. Hurlbut Jnr., Thames and Hudson (London) and Random House (New York 1969).
Minerals and Rocks in Colour, J. F. Kirkaldy, Blandford Press (London 1963).
Minerals, Rocks and Gemstones, Rudolf Borner, Oliver & Boyd (Edinburgh) and Dufour (Chester Springs, Pennsylvania 1962).
The Mineral Kingdom, Paul E. Desautels, Hamlyn (London 1969).
Working with Gemstones, V. A. Firsoff, David and Charles (Newton Abbot Devon 1974).
The Art of the Lapidary, F. J. Sperisen, Bruce Publishing Co. (Milwaukee USA 1950).

Australian Publications

Australian Gem Hunters' Guide, K. J. Buchester, Ure Smith (1965).
Australian Lapidary Guide, K. J. Burchester, Ure Smith (1967).
Australian Rocks, Minerals, Gemstones, R. O. Chalmers, Angus and Robertson (1967).
The Opal Book, Frank Leechman, Ure Smith (1961).
How to find Australian Gemstones, Derrick and Doug Stone, Periwinkle (1969).
Minerals, Rocks and Gems—a Handbook for Australia, J. A. Talen, Jacaranda (1970).
New Zealand Gemstones, L. and R. Cooper, A. H. and A.W. Reed, Wellington, Auckland and Sydney (1969).

Lapidary Magazines

Gems, (bi-monthly) Lapidary Publications, 29 Ludgate Hill, London EC4.
Gemcraft, (monthly) Model & Allied Publications Ltd., P.O. Box 35, Bridge Street, Hemel Hempstead, Herts., England.
Gems and Minerals, (monthly) Gemac Corporation, P.O. Box 687, Mentone, California, USA.
Lapidary Journal, (monthly) P.O. Box 80937, San Diego, California, USA.
Rock and Gem, (bi-monthly) Behn-Miller Publishers Inc., 16250 Ventura Blvd., Encino, California, USA.
The Canadian Rockhound, (bi-monthly) 941 Wavertree Road, North Vancouver, British Columbia, Canada.
Australian Lapidary Magazine, (bi-monthly) Jay Kay Publications, 11 Robinson Street, Sydney, N.S.W., Australia.

Suppliers

Suppliers of lapidary equipment and materials

United Kingdom

Ammonite Ltd, Llandow, Cowbridge, Glamorgan, Wales
M. L. Beach (Products) Ltd, 41 Church Street, Twickenham, Middlesex
Caverswall Minerals, The Dams, Caverswall, Stoke-on-Trent, Staffs.
Craftorama, 14 Endell Street, London WC2
Gemrocks Ltd, 7 Brunswick Shopping Centre, London WC1
Derwent Crafts, 50 Stonegate, York
Gemset of Broadstairs Ltd, 31 Albion Street, Broadstairs, Kent
Gemstones Limited, 44 Walmsley Street, Hull, North Humberside
Glenjoy Lapidary Supplies, 19/21 Sun Lane, Wakefield, Yorkshire
Hirsh Jacobson Merchandising Co. Ltd, 91 Marylebone High Street, London W1
Kernowcraft Rocks & Gems Ltd, 44 Lemon Street, Truro, Cornwall
Manchester Minerals, 33 School Lane, Heaton Chapel, Stockport, Cheshire
A. Massie & Son, 158 Burgoyne Road, Sheffield 6, Yorkshire
PMR Lapidary Equipment & Supplies, Pitlochry, Perthshire, Scotland
Rough and Tumble Ltd, 3 Tyne Street, North Shields, Northumberland
Scotrocks Partners, 48 Park Road, Glasgow C4, Scotland
Barbara Snelling, 349 Lymington Road, Highcliffe, Dorset
Sutherland Gemcutters, Achmelvich by Lairg, Sutherland, Scotland
Thompson & Beevers Limited, St. Just in Penwith, Cornwall
Tideswell Dale Rock Shop, Tideswell, Derbyshire
Wessex Gems and Crafts, Longacre, Downs Road, South Wonston, Winchester, Hants.

USA

Allcraft, 22 West 48th Street, New York, New York 10036
American Handicraft Company, Inc., 20 West 14th Street, New York, New York 10011
Anchor Tool and Supply Company, Inc., 12 John Street, New York, N.Y. 10038
Anoziro Jewelers, 4002 North Stone Avenue, P. O. Box 3988, Tucson, Ariz. 85718
Baldwin-Taylor Hardware & Rock Shop, 4301 Jefferson Highway, New Orleans, Louisiana 70121
Diamond Pacific Tool Corporation, 24063 W. Main Street, Barstow, CA 92311
Geode Industries, 106–108 W. Main, Highway 34, New London, Iowa 52645
Geode Industries, Inc., 107 West Main Street, New London, Iowa 52645
Gilman's, Hellertown, PA. 18055
International Gem, 15 Maiden Lane, New York, New York 10038
Lapribrade Inc., 8 East Eagle Road, Havertown, Pennsylvania 19083
Lapidary Center, 4114 Judah Street, San Francisco, California 94122
Highland Park Manufacturing (Division of Musto Industries Inc.), 12600 Chadron Avenue, Hawthorne, California 90250
Lortone Division of the Carborundum Company, Seattle, Washington 98107
MDR Manufacturing Co. Inc., 4853 Jefferson Blvd., Los Angeles, Cal. 90016

Index